LEWISBURG
1 9 3 7 0

By Lee Miskin

Copyright © 2007 Devira Press

ALL RIGHTS RESERVED. Written permission must be secured from the publisher to use or reproduce any part of this book, except for brief representations in critical reviews or articles.

Published by Devira Press, Nashville TN

Miskin, Lee, 1929 -
    Lewisburg 19370
    ISBN 978-0-6151-5075-8

Printed in the United States of America.

DEDICATION:

To my sister Reba, without whose prodding over many years this book would never have been written.

The following accounts and facts related in this book are true to the best of my knowledge and memory, although many names have been changed for a variety of reasons.

Lee Miskin

INTRODUCTION

The United States Federal Penitentiary at Lewisburg, Pennsylvania in the early 1950's probably contained the most unusual group of federal prisoners ever assembled in one prison. World War II had only been over for five years. There were men serving time who were convicted of treason for aiding the Nazis in World War II. There were many men who were military prisoners serving life sentences for crimes committed during World War II, and busloads of new military prisoners were coming in from the Korean War. These men were young and bitter and probably were the most troublesome of all the inmates.

At the same time in our history as the Korean War, we were going through the height of the "Cold War" between the United States and Russia. This period also coincided with the peak of the era of Joseph McCarthy, the junior senator from the state of Wisconsin. During the hysteria of McCarthyism, a large number of left wing prisoners were put behind the walls in federal prisons and particularly in Lewisburg. Two of the top eleven Communists convicted under the Smith Act were there – John Williamson and Carl Winters – as was Alger Hiss, whose inquisition catapulted Richard Nixon eventually into the Presidency. William Remington was also there and scores of lesser known Communists and left wingers. David Greenglass and Harry Gold, the infamous atomic spies, were in Lewisburg at this time. In addition to this mixed bag of men, there was the usual assortment of federal prisoners: bank robbers, counterfeiters, dope smugglers, illegal aliens, income tax violators, men convicted of white collar business crimes, small time thieves who had crossed state lines, violators of laws governing the U.S. Post Office, Indians from the reservations, and convicted felons from the U.S. territories of Hawaii, Alaska, the Virgin Islands, American Samoa, and Guam. There were also diamond smugglers and big city hoodlums involved in truck hijacking, extortion, illegal gambling, and white slavery across state lines. A very large group of men came from Washington, D.C. simply because the District of Columbia is not a state and has very limited prison facilities. The D.C. prison authorities turned over to the federal government all of their troublemakers in addition to those convicted of federal crimes.

Prison is a horror story, but it is also an education. Serving time with the amalgam of inmates in Lewisburg was more than an education for me. It was a constant exposure to the most diversified elements that an individual can learn from – to learn the worst and to learn the best.

SURVIVAL IN PRISON

In Lewisburg, the Catholics had a full time Catholic chaplain and the Protestants a full time Protestant chaplain. Because of the small number of Jewish inmates, there was no full time Jewish chaplain. A visiting rabbi from a nearby town came in when he could. The Jewish services on Saturday mornings were conducted by the Jewish inmates themselves. The rabbi visited with us on Sundays periodically, mainly to give what comfort he could and to help wherever possible. Although we had no full time chaplain, we had a Jewish leader who was elected through a democratic process under the supervision of the rabbi. This elected leader became the *de facto* leader of the Jewish community in Lewisburg for all purposes, religious and otherwise.

It was in the otherwise category that my judgment and skills, as the leader of the Jewish group, became a matter of life or death – as when one of the Jewish inmates got into serious trouble with either another inmate or an officer. Usually the leadership meant seeing to the wellbeing and welfare of the Jewish group in a very hostile atmosphere.

As every new inmate was admitted to Lewisburg, he filled out various forms and questionnaires. One of the questions asked was about the inmate's religion. It was up to each individual Jew to make the decision for himself whether he wanted to state on the questionnaires that he was Jewish. Some put "no religion." Many felt that the problems of survival in a federal penitentiary would be difficult enough without having the added burden of being officially classified a Jew. Having no chaplain of our own, we came under the jurisdiction of the Protestant chaplain. It was understood that I, as leader of the Jewish inmates, had total authority in the area of our religious observance, and the Protestant chaplain would only assist me if his assistance was needed.

Whenever a Jewish inmate would arrive in Lewisburg and state that he was Jewish, this fact would be forwarded to the Protestant chaplain and he would notify me of the man's name and serial number. Any new arrival in Lewisburg was put in a thirty-day quarantine area, segregated from the rest of the prison population, and given medical, psychological, and educational tests. I would visit these new inmates individually and invite each one to join our Saturday and Sunday services, which in spite of being in quarantine, they were allowed to attend. It was at this point that I would brief them on what prison life was like.

My first question would be, "Have you done time before?" Occasionally, they would say "yes" and then I would tell them that I would assume that there was no need for me to explain prison life to them. I would tell them that if there was anything they wanted to know or if they needed assistance, to contact me. To the men who had not been in prison before, I gave the benefit of my considerable knowledge of the way of life that was now theirs.

The average Jewish prisoner was middle-aged or older, was in prison for some business connected crime, and had never before had intimate contact with the criminal element. These men were in for a great shock because the code of conduct civilized men lived by no longer existed for them. They were in a jungle now that had its own rules, its own code of ethics, its own do's and don'ts. There was no preparation in their past lives for what they now had to face. The rules and conduct in prison have absolutely nothing to do with logic. Generally speaking, the prisoners are cruel, bored, selfish, evil, uneducated men.

I would start by advising, "Don't make any friends, but more importantly, don't make any enemies." This always came as a shock. They could understand why you shouldn't make enemies, but they were unable to comprehend why they shouldn't make friends. I explained it to them as best I could. When someone in prison makes friends with you, usually he will offer his friendship for sexual reasons or for favors he feels he can receive from you. If he asks a favor of you and you don't do it, you have then made an enemy. If you comply with his request and do the favor, in all probability you will wind up in trouble with either the officials of the institution or another inmate. On the other hand, if you have a friend and you ask him to do you a favor and he complies, then he has set you up so that you can't refuse to do him a favor that he is going to ask of you in the future.... And you have the same problem all over again. A smart convict makes no enemies and damn few friends. He keeps his mouth shut, talks to very few people, and then most of the time only when spoken to, and keeps his answers and his conversation limited. It is even unwise to listen, because frequently many things are overheard he is better off not knowing.

The inmates in a prison are liked caged animals. Everyone walks around like a bottle of TNT ready to blow up at any time. An inmate lives a life of total emotional starvation in every aspect. He is deprived of all normal sexual outlets; he is deprived of the normal outlet of getting angry. To show anger in such a charged atmosphere might be the spark that would make the TNT explode. An inmate becomes a controlled robot. The only method of survival is through humor, where and as you can find it. Because of the need for an emotional outlet, a keen sense of humor develops.

If a man comes to prison and makes the wrong moves initially, he has troubles from there on in. A frequent method of the "rat packs" – and they sense their "fish" like trained psychologists – is to create an incident. Shortly after a new inmate's arrival these rat packs will send two or three thugs to jump him and threaten to cut his throat. Next, they have one of their colleagues come in and rescue the victim. The rescuer tells the would-be victim, "Don't worry about those punks. I will look out for you. I will make damn sure that they don't bother you anymore and I will be your friend." The rat pack has now set up the innocent newcomer. He is petrified and he feels he owes his survival to his newfound "friend." His newfound friend now owns him 100%, for whatever purpose he wishes – for sex, or as a supplier of cartons of cigarettes. Frequently he will have the would-be victim's family send monthly checks to the "friend's" associates. This type of extortion is much more prevalent in the prison systems than has ever been publicized by the press. The prisoner lives in constant fear for the rest of his days in prison.

  My job as leader of the Jewish group was to make sure that none of my people fell into such a situation. This was a delicate balancing act at all times. The general inmate population was broken down into three main groups – the black group, the hillbilly group, and the Italian group. The Jewish group was so small as to be insignificant in the power struggles amongst the larger groups, but because of the placement of our men in various sensitive jobs in the institution, we had a position of power which far exceeded our actual numbers.

The blacks had a formalized leadership and their spokesman had great authority. The Italians also had a leader to whom I could speak and who had power over his group. The hillbillies had no organization. They consisted of many splinter groups. The Jews, who were not considered a danger to any of the three major groups, could move in and out and attempt to settle many misunderstandings which could have been blown out of proportion and cause murder, knifings, or an uprising. We had Jews in the education department, in the hospital, in the parole office, and in many secretarial positions. We were able to communicate rapidly with one another. What we lacked in numbers we made up for in influence with the leaders of the various groups who might call on us for assistance.

My position as leader of the Jewish group was enhanced tremendously by two other positions I also held. I was chairman of the debating group, which met weekly for intramural debates, and several times during the year debated with visiting college teams. This gave me the opportunity to meet anyone I wanted in the library, at any time, supposedly to discuss subjects scheduled for debate. In reality, frequently I was working out a serious problem between one of my Jews and some other inmate. In the summer everyone would go out in the recreation yard each evening and on weekends, so communication between inmates was no problem. During the rest of the year, however, we were generally confined and rapid communication was a tricky business that had to be worked on each occasion.

My job as secretary-clerk and assistant to the electric shop foreman was my third area of influence. Initially this post was an insignificant clerk's job which I built into an empire. I learned shortly after being assigned to the job that my boss was a very kind man, very qualified as a mechanic in the electrical field, but that he had no desire or aptitude for the bookkeeping and office work involved in his department. He learned to like, respect, and trust me, and after a short while I was running the whole show. The fewer problems and headaches he had the better he liked it. If he knew there was an electrical problem in some part of the institution that the average inmate-electrician couldn't fix, he would take his crew and do the job with no concern about how the office was being run.

I soon realized that every part of the institution, which is a complete mini-city housing between twelve hundred and fifteen hundred men, had some type of machinery or equipment that needed maintenance or repair from our office. We had electronic lock systems throughout the institution; the hospital had many machines that used electricity; the kitchen also had many machines. The offices of the officials had need for us because of the lighting systems. Even the exterior wall with the floodlights needed our attention. There was, in truth, no part of the reservation, including the farm on the outside of the wall, which was not constantly calling us for assistance or repairs or replacements. When you have a limited number of qualified electricians and a limited budget for new parts and equipment, priorities must be set up. Some requests for service get taken care of and some don't and I was in a position to make these determinations. Inmates never call inmates to have repairs of this type done – it is done by prison officials calling other prison officials. Since my boss was seldom in the office, it became my decision. The officials who run a prison are no different than the civilians who run factories or other businesses. They want and need certain things done to facilitate their jobs. They are very pleased when then get cooperation.

There was another factor which enhanced the power of my job, which struck closer to home for these officials. Most of the top officials lived in government housing outside the walls on the reservation. The prison furnished them with electric stoves and refrigerators. Obviously, any repairs that these items needed would come through my office, and obviously, this put the officials in a position where they would prefer to have a friendly relationship with me than not.

The taboos and approved method of conduct in a prison are so alien to life on the outside that even intelligent, well-meaning inmates to whom I had given my advice upon arrival, would make bad mistakes on their first few days.

One of the most serious types of misconduct is to be seen talking to an officer alone. A new inmate is afraid and he is lonely. When he sees a man in a uniform there is a natural desire to develop some kind of rapport with him. But you cannot do this. Immediately you are marked as a potential informer. The officials of a prison are considered the enemy by the inmates and, therefore, any show of friendship, even a casual conversation between an inmate and an official is very suspect. The interesting thing is that, in actuality, the officials in a prison are not the enemy. It is a very rare circumstance when an official wants to do an inmate harm. The official is a man who works for a modest salary, who wants as few problems as possible during his workday, and who sincerely appreciates any inmate who does not create problems for him.

The real enemy of the inmate is his fellow inmate. By and large they are without decency, without respect for anything or anybody, and with only one fear – the fear of being physically hurt themselves. It is a tremendously difficult psychological adjustment for a new inmate to face these prison realities. He must pretend that the officials are the enemy even though he is surrounded by the slime of civilization. Yet, he must never, never show that he considers the other inmates to be slime. He must project the feeling that he considers the other inmates to be his brothers and the guards to be the enemy.

It is a difficult, very difficult feat of tightrope walking – don't offend the other inmates; don't antagonize the officials; don't be friendly to the officials; make few friends and no enemies within the inmate population.

There are generally two types of inmates in a prison. Every thought and every action of type number one is aimed at enhancing the prospects for his early release. The other type is either a repeater who knows there is no chance of parole, or a long-termer whose day of parole is so far off as not to be considered. The inmate who is constantly concerned about parole sometimes is so frightened of getting involved in anything that might adversely affect his chances for early release that his fear makes him vulnerable. He falls victim to any evil scheme that his fellow inmates might set up for him. The repeater and the long-termer don't think about parole or early release. Their main pastime is the fun of tormenting other prisoners, and establishing the macho image of leadership. These men have nothing in life except their prestige with their fellow cobras. Dealing with men of this type is an unbelievably difficult task. If they are challenged openly, the threat to their prestige is of such importance to them that they feel compelled to murder, knife, or harm their challenger in some way to prove to their colleagues that they are men who cannot be trifled with. If weakness is shown to these individuals, they will pursue their goal with the glee of a demon – just to watch and enjoy the suffering they inflict. That is why in prison the world's greatest diplomacy in practiced – it is much more of an art than that used by our State Department career officers.

Middlemen are needed to go between the various groups and smooth out difficulties before they reach the point of explosion. My position was such that not only did inmates come to me to solve problems, but many times officials would seek me out. They gave me no details, but told me that one of my men was having a problem with someone in one of the other groups and they suggested I straighten it out. First, I would have to contact the man in question and get from him an honest answer as to what was going on. It is an interesting fact that in the evil, charged atmosphere of prison, honesty between my fellow Jews and myself on sensitive issues was never a problem. They were aware that their very survival could well depend on the completeness and accuracy of the story they told me.

If one of the black or Italian groups were involved in the difficulty with my man, I would send word through an intermediary to the leader of the group. We would meet at a certain place and at a certain time so that we could talk. These leaders held their positions because they protected their men as I protected mine. They knew that regardless of the cause for the bad relations, if the situation exploded, it would affect the welfare of everybody. It was always to the benefit of all concerned to keep things calm. When the problem involved someone outside the black or Italian groups, and there was no official leadership involved, it became much more tricky to work things out. You would have to find out through intermediaries who knew other intermediaries if there was anyone who had influence on the individual involved. Many times this entailed several meetings with several people, and along the way we would find someone who owed someone a favor. Through this method, generally speaking, I kept the Jews in my group out of major problems.

Physical survival is only one aspect. Emotional and mental survival are equally as important and much more difficult to maintain. In contrast to what the public would assume, I maintain that the less contact an inmate has with the outside world the better off he is. I mean this specifically in terms of letters and visits from his loved ones. The most difficult time for an inmate is his first few months. That is because he is still mentally and emotionally living on the outside. As a defense mechanism, he refuses to accept the fact that his whole world exists within the prison walls. It is too harsh a reality to accept. Therefore, he will use any possible means to delude himself that he is only a temporary resident, with total disinterest in the activities within the walls. This is the time when men are constantly talking about new trials, or getting out on appeal. They live each day with hope that the following day will bring news. Each day they suffer hour by hour. Many people wonder how it is possible for a man doing a long sentence or even a lifer to adjust to his circumstances. They don't understand and cannot understand that it is much easier for these men than the men on very short sentences. A man with a long sentence who has been confined for a number of years realizes that the prison is his home and his world, and he adapts himself.

The importance of separating the outside world from the reality of living inside the walls is perhaps shown at its sharpest when two men develop a close friendship. You see them together constantly. They eat together, work together, and run the track together, or play handball together. In the winter, when the recreation yard is not available, you will see these men in the library together, or just sitting and talking in the inside recreational facilities. It might be assumed by many people that a relationship of this type would have sexual overtones. That is not so, and their fellow inmates have the psychological ability to know when it is true and when it is not true. An inmate is a keen and astute observer, to an extent that he himself is not aware of.

When one of these inseparable friends makes parole and has only sixty to ninety days to do before release, a startling change takes place. The two friends no longer have anything in common. The man who has not made parole doesn't want to be around the man who did. His life must continue on in the daily routine as before, and he doesn't want to and can't afford to have discussions about the outside world. If he were to spend much time with his former close friend listening to stories of his family, friends, and his new life, without realizing it, he could develop a strong hatred towards the friend, out of uncontrollable jealousy. The man who has made parole understands this and will seek an entire new set of friends. His friends will be those other men who have also made parole or men who have a very short time left on their sentences. They have much in common. The institution they live in now becomes meaningless and all their thoughts and emotions are focused on the day of their release. It is not uncommon that when a man receives his parole and has from thirty to ninety days left, he will voluntarily request the warden to have him checked into solitary confinement. Solitary confinement, as most people understand it, is used only for punishment and is a very harsh way of life. When a man voluntarily asks for this, he must have a damn good reason. In this case his reason is very simple. He has survived the barbarity of prison life and now his day of release is near. He is afraid that he might receive some kind of disciplinary action and violate his parole, or wind up in a fight with another inmate, which could violate his parole, or even worse, get him hurt or killed.

Thus, if he is placed in solitary confinement, he is guaranteed that he will walk out of prison on his scheduled day of release.

Once an inmate accepts the fact that his life within the walls is his only life, he develops certain mental games since his activities are extremely restricted. Everything becomes magnified far beyond its actual proportions. The slightest denial of something he has been looking forward to is considered a disaster. If the movie doesn't show up on Saturday night, if a change to a new cellblock is delayed, if he doesn't get a new pair of pants to replace his torn ones, it becomes a traumatic experience. The small disappointments become very large. On the other hand, the human mind adapts to allow a person to survive because this same person will get extreme pleasure and happiness from the most minor development. An unexpected good meal, when he had anticipated the usual unappetizing food, becomes a thrilling event. Not that the food he is eating is so great, but because it is better than what he has been eating and what he expected to eat. A holiday meal, such as on the Fourth of July, Christmas, or New Year's, becomes a truly gala event. A new pair of shoes is treated with great affection. A joke is appreciated with laughter that you couldn't imagine on the outside. Entertainers are always extremely gratified when they entertain behind prison walls because of the reception they are given by the inmates. They can't fathom the meaning their performance has for the inmates. It is not just the talents and ability of the performer that are so appreciated. It is an opportunity to forget for a few moments where they are.

Most men in prison learn to control their minds to the point of not thinking about the outside world. However, every inmate reaches a point in his sentence when he becomes eligible for parole. Regardless of his record inside the prison or his previous convictions as a felon, he still has a chance. Once this glimmer of hope reaches the inmate, he becomes a different person. He no longer can control himself to think of the prison as his only world. Gradually, day by day, the thoughts of release and the world outside sneak into his mind. Finally, he is sent up to his caseworker's office and he is handed a notice. If he has made parole, his caseworker will discuss many aspects of his release with him. If he has not made parole, he will be handed his parole application with a big rubber stamp across the top, saying, "DENIED." This is a point at which many a stable man has fallen to pieces. All of his carefully prepared emotional shields have collapsed.

Psychologically, he is on the edge of a precipice and he is very unpredictable. The grapevine in any prison is one of the best communication systems in the world and in a very short time everyone knows who has been turned down for parole. It is an unwritten rule amongst the inmates that you do not speak to a man that has missed parole. You don't get close to him. You give him plenty of room in the corridors, in the cellblocks, and in the recreation yard. You speak to him only when he speaks to you. He is a stick of dynamite that could blow up at any time and take you along with him. Some adjust to denial of parole in a short time and return to their normal ways in the life of the prison. Other men take much longer. Some men never make the adjustment. When an inmate is ready to reenter the normal prison routine, he doesn't have to make any announcements. He just starts in doing what he used to do and talking to the other inmates. Rarely do inmates make a mistake as to when a man is ready for the old routine.

The mental anguish that is a constant has its cycles, and each man knows how to protect himself when he feels a downer coming on. The best way is to speak to no one and the inmates recognize this. They can read it in a man's face, and they can smell it. They leave these people alone because the wrong word at the wrong time could turn one into a maniac.

The unvarying routine of prison life causes a degree of boredom that strains a person's mental stability. Outlets are so limited that it drives men into unbelievably complex schemes to outwit the officials. Men can plan for weeks and months, utilizing the timing of a commando raid, to accomplish no more than to smuggle a loaf of bread out of the kitchen. It is the thrill of the victory that makes the effort worthwhile. I have seen men on the verge of a nervous breakdown improve overnight after an injury. They now had something physical to think about and to distract them. They can feel the cast on their leg, touch their bandaged arm, and watch their damaged body mend and heal. I have learned that caring for the body can save the mind.

KOHEN WITH A "K"

The first time I met Kohen with a K, he was still in quarantine. He was a short, fat man with broad shoulders, a very large nose, thinning hair, an infectious smile, and a voice that combined a Jewish accent with New York Brooklynese. He was in his middle sixties. On his first visit to our services I introduced him to the rest of the congregation and I said, "This is Emiss Kohen, with a K." From then on, throughout his stay in Lewisburg he was known to one and all, both the inmates and the officers, as Kohen with a K.

Kohen with a K was in for a short sentence of eighteen months because of some business fraud in the fur market in which he was involved in New York City. He was a devoutly religious man, very knowledgeable in Hebrew and religious observances and procedures. In his heart he was a gentle man, but he had a very undiplomatic and rough manner of speaking. He could antagonize an angel in a very short discussion. He thought he knew everything about everything, and in spite of his size and his age, he had fear of no man. When I tried to explain to him the proper method of conduct in prison, he laughed.

He said, "Miskin, I have been handling punks like these all my life. Don't worry about me. I can take care of myself."

He was given a job in the kitchen because he had grown up working in his family's restaurant in Brooklyn. From the day he started work he was a troublemaker. Not only did he constantly raise hell with the inmates for not preparing the food properly, but he even scolded the officials. He was annoyed with the officials because they didn't know enough about food, they weren't watching the inmates, and they really didn't give a damn since they didn't have to eat the food. In truth, there was a separate officer's mess and all the cooking was done separately for the officers. After the first day in the kitchen, reports came back to me that I should have a talk with Kohen with a K. I explained it to him.

I said, "Kohen with a K, you can't do that in jail." I said, "Look, you have got to mind your own business, do what they tell you to do, and keep your mouth shut."

He said, "Miskin, I appreciate your interest in me. But I know what I am doing. I cannot work in a kitchen and watch them ruin the food."

I said, "Kohen with a K, you are new here, damn it, listen to what I tell you."

He said, "O.K. Miskin, I know you mean good. I will try to behave myself."

It was only two days later that I got a request from one of the officials asking me to have a talk with Kohen with a K because he was embarrassing the officers assigned to the supervision of the kitchen crew. I was told that if he continued, disciplinary action would be taken against him. Again, I contacted him.

I said, "Kohen with a K, you are giving me problems. I got a report that you told the head steward in front of the inmates that he wasn't cooking something right and it tasted terrible. Goddamn it, who are you to open your mouth and tell them what to do? You could be in a world of trouble. You could stay in isolation for weeks. This is your first time in prison. Probably you will make parole if you behave yourself. You have a wife and family waiting for you. Goddamn it, keep your mouth shut."

He said, "You are right, Miskin. I appreciate your interest in me. But I just can't stand by and watch them ruin good food. I see the food when they bring it in. It's good food, but it tastes like *drek* when they finish cooking it."

Things were quiet for the next two weeks. Then I got a message from the leader of the Italian group that he wanted to see me. We set up a meeting in the recreation yard. This was a man who had total control of his group. He was very respected, a man in his middle thirties who was doing twenty years for counterfeiting. As I approached him, he was with his two lieutenants. As was the custom when you had an appointment, they stopped walking and allowed their leader and me to talk privately. They followed about ten paces to the rear.

Mario said to me, "Miskin, we have got a problem."

I said, "What is it, Mario?"

He said, "You know one of your boys named Kohen with a K?"

I said, "Unfortunately, I know him well.

What's he gotten into now?"

He said, "One of my boys in the kitchen has threatened to kill him."

I said, "What happened?"

He went on in great detail to explain to me that Kohen with a K had told his man how to cook a particular kind of food and his man told Kohen with a K to go to hell and mind his own business. Whereupon, Kohen with a K, thinking he was back on the streets of Brooklyn, called the officer nearby and told him that this inmate was messing up his food. Anyone who has been in prison for even one day knows the unwritten law – that you never call a guard and cause trouble for another inmate. It so happened that this particular inmate had been in Lewisburg for at least ten years and he was facing parole shortly. He had already had several disciplinary actions against him and he felt for sure that this little incident might cause him to miss parole. He had already sent word out that Kohen with a K was a marked man. Mario went on to explain that his boy was a good boy with a good family back in New York. He didn't want any problems for him. The proposition that Mario gave me was that he would take care of his boy if I would take care of my boy.

He said, "I don't care how you do it, just tell your man, Kohen with a K, that if he ever puts his finger on any of my boys again, he is a dead man. And meanwhile, I will use my influence to quiet down the whole thing."

I, of course, knew the seriousness of the situation and I explained to Mario that he was right one hundred percent in everything he said. "However," I told him, "Kohen with a K is an old man. He is a stupid man. He has a big mouth. He has never been in jail before and he is too damn dumb and hardheaded to realize what is right and what is not right to do. He happens to be a dedicated man for good food, and he means no harm. He is not an informer, because I understand that when he went to trial on his fur business conviction, he involved no one else with him."

I assured Mario that I would take care of Kohen with a K. I told him that I appreciated his coming to me first and if there was anything I could do for him in the future, to please let me know. I knew that what had been presented to me was not an idle threat.

I was aware that the image of the total Italian prison population was at stake. Everyone was waiting to see how the rat that had called in a guard would be handled. I also understood that Mario did have the authority to stop any trouble. And I further understood that for his own purposes and for the benefit of the men under him, he didn't want a murder and F.B.I. investigators coming inside the walls. I also knew that he would be coming to me in the future for a favor, but that was part of the game.

My only problem was what in the hell to do with Kohen with a K. I met Kohen with a K that same day in the Protestant chaplain's office because it was too much of an emergency situation to wait for the following day in the recreation yard. The Protestant chaplain was usually very considerate and helpful when I told him I wanted to use his office for a special prayer. So, here comes Kohen with a K into the chaplain's office. I looked at him, patted him on his cheek, shook his hand, and said, "Kohen with a K, what the hell am I going to do with you?"

Like a little boy, he hung his head because he knew there were problems. I didn't go into any details about the meeting I had, because I couldn't trust him. He wouldn't deliberately place me in trouble in any way, but he was so illogical and emotional, he might say things without thinking. The best way I could, I explained to him the danger that he was in for what he'd done.

His answer was, "They can't scare me. I've been dealing with punks like that all my life."

I talked to him for maybe two hours, explaining to him the sensitivity of the situation. The only way I could reach him was by convincing him that if something happened to him it would involve the total Jewish population of the institution and that the ramifications would be harmful to me and to the job I was trying to do. All the Jewish friends he had made at the services who wanted no trouble, no problems, and who wanted to get out as soon as possible on parole to join their families, would be put in jeopardy. I begged him as a personal favor to me and for the good work I was doing, and for the sake of the other Jewish inmates, to please keep his mouth shut and do his job, and no more.

He said, "For you, I'll do it. The first thing tomorrow, I'll go up to that bum and apologize to him."

I said, "No, Kohen with a K. That is not the way you do it. In jail you don't call a guard to tell on an inmate and then after you have done it, you don't apologize."

He said, "What do you want me to do, Miskin?"

I said, "What I want you to do is to be a good boy. Don't talk unless you are spoken to and when you speak, make it short and quiet, and mind your own damn business."

He said, "For you I'll do it, Miskin."

And, temporarily, Kohen with a K stayed out of trouble.

HARRY GOLD
19312

    The secrets of the atomic bomb were stolen from the United States government at Los Alamos, New Mexico and handed over to the Soviet Union. Harry Gold, David Greenglass, and Ethel and Julius Rosenberg were the perpetrators of the deed that sent shock waves around the world. The Rosenbergs died in the electric chair in Sing Sing Prison, New York. David Greenglass, who was Ethel's brother, and Harry Gold were sent to Lewisburg Federal Penitentiary.

    Harry Gold pleaded guilty before Judge James P. McGrannery in Philadelphia. He had cooperated with the F.B.I. in the Rosenberg case and in all other espionage cases that were pending. He was sentenced to thirty years in a federal penitentiary. Judge McGrannery later became the U.S. Attorney General.

    I first met Harry when we were both in the quarantine area of Lewisburg, where all newcomers spend thirty days isolated from the general prison population. He was a small, quiet man. He acknowledged his guilt, and he carried his guilt with him constantly, like a heavy weight on his back. He was a very intelligent and sensitive man, and his past deeds ate away at him like a cancer. He and I became very close over the next five year period that I knew him. He never spoke of his misdeeds with other inmates, but he opened his heart to me, I think, because he felt that I truly pitied him and wished him well. He had been a Soviet agent for many years. He asked me once, "How do you get off a tiger's back?" He didn't expect forgiveness for what he had done, but, like all of us, he needed someone to whom he could pour out his heart.

Harry Gold was a chemist by profession, and he had worked for the Franklin Sugar Company in Philadelphia for many years. The officials in Lewisburg utilized his abilities and assigned him to work in the hospital laboratory. To this job he devoted his life. It was his emotional outlet, and when he wasn't in his cell, he was there. He felt that the inmates in the hospital were his personal responsibility, and there was nothing that he wouldn't do for their welfare. A team of doctors was sent to Lewisburg from the National Institutes of Health in Washington, D.C. to do experimental work in hepatitis, using inmate volunteers as their guinea pigs.

Harry not only assisted the doctors with their laboratory work, but he took the experimental injections himself.

Harry was not married, but David Greenglass told me on several occasions that Harry had a girlfriend of many years. He never had visits from her and he never spoke of her, and I never asked.

It was only after many years at Lewisburg that Harry started going out to the recreation yard, where he played chess for long hours. He didn't enjoy any type of physical exercise. He once told me about his college days. He was forced to participate in some type of sport, and he chose fencing because he thought it would be the least strenuous of the sports offered. He soon found out that of all the college sports, fencing demanded the most physical fitness conditioning. He worked like a demon for weeks before he even tried to use a foil.

In the circumstances that Harry and I lived and talked, year after long year, there is not much that one man can hide from another. The veil that most people wear all their lives is lifted, and the true person shows, for better or for worse. You get to know the essence of a man. The facts of Harry's past life became unimportant to me. He was a gentle, kind, warm, compassionate person. Many people in Lewisburg hated him for what he had done, but no one had anything but kind feelings for Harry Gold, the man.

One day while he was walking through the grassy area of the baseball field, on the way to play his chess game, Harry came across a tiny infant rabbit. Although it was not common practice to see rabbits within the walls of Lewisburg, it was not that unique either, because there was, on the other side of the wall, a large prison farm with many small animals roaming around. Periodically, some small animal would run inside. The rules in a federal penitentiary are very strict about having a pet of any kind, including a bird that might fly into a man's cell, but Harry decided that he needed a friend. He put the tiny rabbit in his pocket and carried it back to his cell after the recreation period was over.

It is important to understand the tight security that exists within a federal prison. Not only are cells and work areas checked periodically and at odd times, but the men themselves are physically searched many times during the day to try to find contraband. It was a very complex logistical problem for Harry to constantly take his rabbit with him from his cell to the hospital laboratory through several checkpoints. While he had the rabbit with him at the laboratory, he had to watch him, clean him, and feed him.

As a chemist, Harry was aware of the nutritional needs of his rabbit and he knew what type of food to procure for him. Harry could take care of most of the rabbit's needs by stealing small quantities of food from the mess hall or asking friends to bring scraps of food. There was one ingredient that he felt the rabbit required which was lacking, and that was fresh clover. The recreation area was heavy with grass, but like most grass, contained only a small amount of clover. Each person could spend only a limited amount of time in the yard, and in order to secure the necessary amount of clover for his ever-growing rabbit, Harry needed considerable help. It was a very difficult favor to ask for assistance in bringing clover into the prison to be used for an illegal purpose. However, the warmth of the story in the bleak prison atmosphere enlisted the aid of many, many men. They walked about the prison yard, picked up a few pieces of clover, and put the clover into their pockets. Then they brought the clover back inside the walls, and by stealth, arranged to get it to Harry. Thus, Harry was able to constantly secure a fresh supply of clover for his rabbit friend.

The initial method of getting the rabbit from his cell to the hospital laboratory, through the various checkpoints, had to be changed from time to time as problems arose. But one problem arose that neither Harry nor anyone else had foreseen. Due to Harry's knowledge of nutrition, and the abundance of clover, the tiny rabbit was growing extremely large. Smuggling a small baby rabbit the size of a tennis ball from place to place is one thing, but hiding a rabbit as big as a basketball becomes much more difficult to achieve. The ingenuity employed and the solutions to the problems that developed are too numerous to describe. He hid him wrapped up in towels that were to be taken to the laundry; he poured trash around him while supposedly emptying trashcans; he wrapped pants around the rabbit with the pretense that he was taking the pants to be mended.

Even with all these schemes, the point was reached when Harry had to make a decision. He was not only involving himself in violations of rules, but as the rabbit got larger and the schemes got more elaborate, he was forced to involve many friends. The thought of having disciplinary action taken against anyone for assisting him is the only factor that made him make an extremely painful decision. He had to give up his deeply loved rabbit friend. Word of his decision was spread around to Harry's friends. Through another series of camouflaged activities, the rabbit was brought out to the yard. As a group of perhaps twenty men walked in a cluster near the rear gate, which was a taboo area, the rabbit was released. It did not, as would be expected, immediately run through the gate. He had to be picked up, walked around, with the group dispersing and then gathering together again. Another try was made at releasing the rabbit near the gate. After about three tries, the rabbit looked back at Harry, and ran through the rear gate into the countryside surrounding Lewisburg.

HOW TO ACQUIRE AN EDUCATION
THE HARD WAY

When I first entered Lewisburg, one of the big question marks in my mind concerned the type of job assignment I would receive. My sentence was four to fourteen years, which meant that I was eligible for parole at the end of four years, but only eligible. The type of work that a man does in prison when he is a long-timer obviously is of great importance to his emotional adjustment and well being in prison. I was twenty-two years old and had seen service in the Army. In the two years since my discharge I had not learned any skills that would be useful in Lewisburg. Generally, a man without a trade is given unpleasant work requiring physical labor. My first assignment was washing pots and pans in the kitchen, a most difficult, tiresome, and unpleasant task. I assumed that the authorities, in their wisdom, had determined that this would be my work for the remainder of my sentence. I didn't realize that new men are usually assigned to unpleasant kitchen chores until such time as the classification committee determines the permanent job.

The results of my educational testing and my I.Q. convinced the committee to send me to school full-time for a period of four months to learn to be a clerk typist. In prison there are many, many tasks that require a typist and the ordinary inmate has had no typing experience. The courses that were taught me were business English, typing, business mathematics, and a smattering of other office skills and information.

It was during this period that I came to appreciate the great educational opportunities available to any inmate in Lewisburg. The clerk typist classes were the only full-time course of study conducted in the institution, because these skills were desperately needed to fill jobs. However, there was an education department that offered courses of every type to all inmates. These courses were taught in the evenings after working hours. Even though we were staffed by a superb group of men, the staff could have been even better. Many of our most able inmates were not allowed to be instructors because of their left wing political activities and convictions.

One of our teachers was Douglas Chandler, a convicted Nazi, who had broadcast for the Germans during World War II. He was an evil man, but a good English teacher. A major general by the name of Myers, who had been convicted for pay-offs under a "five per cent" investigation, taught World War II history. We had many C.P.A. inmates who taught economics and taxation and bookkeeping. Spanish teachers were in plentiful supply from our Puerto Rican contingent. There was an excellent course in psychology, taught by an ex- high school principal. Since a large percentage of our inmates were almost illiterate, there were many courses in basic reading, writing, and arithmetic. The education department in Lewisburg took pride in its annual announcement of how many inmates had received high school diplomas from the State of Pennsylvania.

It was too bad that the number of men receiving diplomas became more important to the officials running the education department than how much these men were actually learning. The education department became a diploma mill. The staff was under constant pressure to recruit more men and to make sure they passed the test required for a diploma. The end result was that the inmate instructors would illegally assist their students in taking the test to insure that each year the number of graduates would exceed that of the previous year. The annual increase looked excellent on the record of the official in charge of the education department, and he showed his appreciation to the inmate instructors. The inmates who received diplomas were also very appreciative because earning a high school diploma looked good on their records. The fact that these men were learning little didn't seem to be relevant.

Even with the shortcomings in the educational system, excellent facilities were available for any man with the determination to take advantage of them. Other than the education department courses, there were many approved correspondence courses that were free to any inmate who applied. Obviously, finding time to study was never a problem.

The most significant facility available for an education is the prison library. We were fortunate in having a well-stocked library at Lewisburg. Regardless of the field of a man's interest, he could find a more than adequate section of books in the library. The library became a magnet for me and I cherished it. It was not only a place to temporarily escape from my prison reality, but it gave purpose to life. Even though my youth was being wasted in the prison environment, my mind was being cultivated and trained. I have no doubt whatsoever that had my time been spent in America's finest universities, I would not have received the education that Lewisburg provided me. Both the books in the library and the pressure cooker prison atmosphere were my school. I feel very strongly that any man who has served several years in a prison with an adequate library can improve himself immeasurably. I used the library not only to gain knowledge in specific fields, but to give myself a generalized education in the many areas I knew I was deficient in.

When I was first assigned to my clerk typist position in the electrical shop, I would sit in the office with nothing to do. I was unfamiliar with my duties and my boss frequently was not in the office. The rules in Lewisburg were that an inmate could not take reading material of any kind to his place of work, but I sidestepped the rule. I took a dictionary from the library and brought it to my office. The first day an official asked what kind of a book I had and I explained that it was a dictionary I needed in my job. No one could possibly object to that. The first few months I spent every spare moment reading the dictionary from front to back.

One evening I was sitting in my cell with my co-defendant, when the door opened suddenly. It was the captain of the guards. I had never seen the captain in our cellblock at night before and I couldn't imagine what he wanted. I invited him in and asked him what the problem was. He said, "No problem. Just continue doing what you were doing."

It was obvious that he had been drinking heavily. I looked at Demetrius and we continued with what we had been doing when he entered. I was reading Shakespeare to my friend and we alternated reading and listening. After some uncomfortable minutes for all concerned, the captain got up and walked out. I never did learn what his purpose was in coming to my cell, but I am quite sure he did not expect to find two inmates reading Shakespeare aloud to each other.

As I advanced through my own personal education, I often looked back to my initial schooling that took place in the clerk typist course. I recall vividly that in the first few weeks I was quite sure I would fail and be thrown out of school. In prison, while being trained for a desirable job, the slow or unproductive students are not tolerated. My problem was that I found learning to type a near impossible task.

Typing was taught in a very simple and basic manner. We were handed an instruction book titled "Rowe Typing." We opened to page one and read the instructions and then attempted to use our fingers on the keyboard as directed in the book. I consider myself an intelligent man, but I rapidly learned that my fingers were stupid. No matter how hard I tried, my fingers would not move to the right keys. It was not a matter of giving up or of taking longer to learn than the other man. My choice was either keep up with the class or go back to washing pots and pans for perhaps the next fourteen years. The harder I tried, the more stupid my fingers became. I was convinced that it was impossible for me to learn to type without looking at the keys and watching my fingers. How could I possibly type with my eyes focused on the reading material?

The process of learning to type has given me the tenacity to learn other difficult things in my life, because for me, learning to type was the most difficult learning process of all. I would sweat like a hog. Beads of sweat would fall off my head onto the paper. My fingers would sweat on the keyboard. They would also freeze on the keyboard. Then, one day, as if by a signal from God, my fingers learned to think. To my complete amazement each finger knew which key it was supposed to jump to, and when I looked at my fingers I saw that they moved around so rapidly, punching the proper keys without my conscious direction. I had conquered the mental block to typing.

I knew that if I could learn to type, nothing else could stand in my way.

A KIND GUARD

Clifford C. Waters was my boss. His friends among the other guards called him Bucky. He was a short man with a well-proportioned body, who had worked hard all of his life in the electrical trade. Rather than the standard issue peaked cap of a prison guard, Walters always wore a baseball cap. The senior officers in Lewisburg didn't approve of his headgear. However, since he was in the maintenance department and always used the excuse that the other type hat hampered his work, they let him get away with it. Walters was a very good electrician. His job was to maintain all the electrical systems in our prison city and he liked his work. His approach to prison life was totally different from that of the men whose job was to enforce the regulations. He liked his men and he treated each one with the respect and friendship that they earned. He was not a dumb man and he was aware of the many, many schemes that the men under him were involved in. However, he pretended not to notice and never took any official actions. Each officer is issued a disciplinary report book, which is known among the inmates as a "shot book." Whenever an inmate violates a rule, the officer in charge issues a disciplinary report, gives a copy to the inmate, and submits the original to the associate warden for disciplinary action. To the best of my knowledge, during the more than five years I worked for and with this man, he never used his book. As a matter of fact, it was a standard joke among the men that the majority of the time he would forget to bring his book with him.

Generally, inmates appreciate a man of Walter's type very much. There is a code of honor among them to do nothing that would put him in the middle and cause his superiors to come down on him. It is understood that inmates will deviate from the rules in any way they can, but no one ever did anything in front of Walters. He could not be accused by another official or an informing inmate that he was aware of a specific violation and did nothing to stop it. Of course, there are some inmates who don't care about the fate or reputation of a prison guard. If it is known to the other inmates that a prisoner has knowingly placed a guard such as Mr. Walters in an embarrassing position, the other inmates will make damn sure that he will not do it again.

Although Walters was an excellent electrician, he was a very poor administrator. He was pleased to have me in the office because I not only did the clerical work but I gradually took charge of the total operation. I assigned men to repair jobs, ordered material and parts, and worked up cost estimates for the larger jobs. Walter learned to have total trust and confidence in me. I finally asked him to submit my name to the warden for reduction in custody so that I could accompany him on jobs outside the walls. He knew as well as I did that it was not necessary for his secretary to go outside the walls on electrical repair jobs. However, he agreed that he would do his best for me. He used as an excuse the fact that I ordered all the parts for machinery and other men would frequently fail to get the correct information from the equipment. He wanted this to be my responsibility. To my great joy I received a reduction from maximum to medium custody, which meant that I could go outside the walls with an officer present.

I had been behind the walls two and a half years the first time Clifford Walters took me outside with him. I shall always remember the excitement and the unexplainable fright I felt at watching the large gates swing open and the guard in the tower direct Walters and me to pass through. When you have seen only the inside of the walls every day for two and a half years, emotionally you begin to feel that the world stops at the walls. The feeling of fright is inconceivable because it is so illogical, but I know that as I walked through the gate I stood very close to Walters. The guard has a picture of each inmate in a rack, and as an inmate passes through he checks the picture against the person to make sure that the right inmate is coming through.

That first day, as I drove with my boss from facility to facility near the farm, I didn't leave his side. He kept telling me, "Don't worry, Miskin. Everything is all right. You wait for me here and I'll come back."

Each time I asked him, "Would you mind if I went with you?"

The fright is illogical because you know you're not doing anything wrong. You know you have legal permission to be where you are. However, being on the other side of the wall, you are in alien territory. It's like being on the moon. I felt comfortable with Walters next to me because I knew that if I were accused of any wrongdoing, he would be there to protect me and to testify that everything was O.K. On the outside of the walls without my boss, I felt like a little boy who has been deserted in the middle of a wild jungle. Of course, gradually, after going through the gate several times, I became accustomed to the experience and soon it became routine. It is the first time that has that terrifying, mystifying effect on you that you can't understand and can't anticipate until it actually happens.

Walters understood the reaction because he had taken inmates through the walls many times and had seen the effect on them. He told me a story of an inmate I knew who had been in Lewisburg for over twenty years. This inmate was a very large and powerful man from the hills of West Virginia. He was very quiet and very respected among the inmates. When Walters took him through the gate about two years before my time, he had been inside for over eighteen years. Walters told me of the unbelievable effect it had on him. As they went through the gate, he grabbed Walters by his arm.

Walters told him, "Everything is all right. Calm down."

He couldn't calm down. He grabbed Walters around his waist and held him in a bear hug. He trembled from head to foot. Walters soothingly explained to him that everything was all right. "Let's sit down and talk about it. There's nothing to get upset about." And they sat down right next to the wall. They didn't leave the wall and the man cried like a baby. He cried and carried on for a long time. Then he asked permission to go back inside. He couldn't take any more that day.

The next day they went out again. He didn't cry and he didn't grab Walters, but he held his hand until he retained his composure. In time, of course, he adjusted like all men have and will. Walters didn't find these human reactions at all humorous. He was a kind man and he realized the suffering the inmates were going through. He did everything within his power to treat these inmates as men and show his appreciation for their good conduct, their effort in their work, and their friendship.

The first time I went outside the walls with Mr. Walters, his kindness to me was all I needed. After I became accustomed to the new experience of freedom, I became aware of the things in the outside world that I didn't see inside.

We grew tomatoes on the prison farm. I mentioned to Mr. Walters how beautiful the tomatoes were. One day he stopped the truck right next to the tomato patch and said, "Miskin, I'm going to smoke a cigarette. Why don't you get out of the truck and stretch your legs for awhile?"

I said, "I don't want to go anywhere."

He said, "Why don't you just sit down next to the truck in the shade where nobody can see you and you'll be right next to those nice tomatoes that are growing over there."

I understood what he was telling me. It was his way never to give you permission to do something that was a violation of the rules. However, he would hint that he would be happy to turn his head the other way if you were inclined to do something. I jumped out of the truck, sat down in the shade, and grabbed a big tomato. I didn't care that it was dirty. I wiped the excess dirt on my pants and bit into the tomato. I had never before in all my life eaten a tomato that was still warm from the sun. It was fresh, and damn it tasted good. I think I ate four or five of them. This became a rather routine thing for us as time went on and the tomatoes ripened. Without saying anything, he would pull the truck over to the side of the road, light up a cigarette, and I would jump out to the tomato patch. I never got tired of the taste of the sun-warmed tomatoes.

All the same, it was late at night when you were trying to go to sleep and feeling depressed that snacking food was missed the most. The rules were very strict about bringing food or anything else through the walls when an inmate was on an outside job detail. Not only did we have to go through an electric eye, which would detect anything metal, but we were given a very thorough hand shakedown to detect anything being brought in.

One day after I had passed through the shakedown with Mr. Walters and we were walking back towards our building, he opened his windbreaker and I saw that he had four apples hidden inside. Without saying a word, he handed them to me and I put them under my shirt. That night when lights were out and all was quiet, there was a loud crunching sound in my cell. This apple incident was repeated many, many times over the years. I never spoke about it and he never spoke about it. That was the way we had with each other. He was a kind man but he did not like to openly violate any of the prison rules. He did what he felt he should do, and then he didn't want to talk about it.

One morning when I had come to work, Walters looked at me for a long time and then he said, "Miskin, I'm going to put you in for M.G.T."

M.G.T. stands for meritorious good time. There are two types of good time – statutory good time and meritorious good time. Any inmate who is sentenced to a federal prison, by law is entitled to a certain number of days per month as time off for good behavior. This means if he does not make parole and must serve the full sentence, his sentence will be reduced by the number of good days accumulated. The amount of good days given per month is strictly related to the total length of a sentence. The longer the sentence, the more days per month an inmate is entitled to. These good days, of course, are subject to the inmate's good behavior, and the officials in any federal prison have the discretionary power to revoke the good days for any violation of prison rules. Loss of good time is a very serious matter because it means that the inmate will not get out before his total sentence is completed. It also means that he can't make parole if he has lost any of his good days.

Meritorious good time is something else. It is not rare for a prisoner to receive it, but it is not commonplace either. The purpose of the extra good time is to encourage inmates to put forth extra effort in their jobs above and beyond the normally required work effort. In actuality, this extra good time is just fluff and has no real meaning if a man makes parole. Most men who receive parole have their parole date set up in advance, supposedly to give them time to prepare themselves for release. The meritorious good time they have accumulated is subtracted from the parole date of release. In actual fact, the release date is juggled so that a man with a large amount of meritorious good days accumulated will have his release date set further back than a man with a small number of days, or no days at all. Naturally, meritorious good time is helpful to any inmate who doesn't make parole and has to serve his full sentence. Since there are very few men who receive meritorious good time and still don't make parole, the biggest benefit of M.G.T. is that it looks good on an inmate's record.

The reason Mr. Walters gave the warden for requesting M.G.T. for me was that I had saved the prison large sums of money. My method of saving money was very simple, but it had not been done in Lewisburg before. Routinely, the General Services Administration in Washington, D.C. and the Defense Department circulated among the various federal agencies pamphlets listing surplus supplies and equipment. Prior to my coming to Lewisburg, very little attention had been paid to these government notices. I realized that there were many electrical supplies listed in the pamphlets that we used constantly in our maintenance, supplies such as electric wire conduit, electrical outlets, and small parts of various kinds. Anything that we ordered from these surplus pamphlets was sent to us without charge. Like all government agencies, we operated on a budget that had to be justified every year. There were always many items we wanted to purchase that we couldn't because of budgetary limitations. Because of the many free surplus items we now routinely received, we were able to purchase new equipment and tools, which we were never able to buy before. Walters felt this was sufficient reason for the board of review, under the warden, to grant me meritorious good time.

Over the years, Mr. Walters eased the burden of imprisonment for many men under his jurisdiction in any way that he could.

DAVID GREENGLASS
19352

The first time I met David Greenglass he, Harry Gold, and I were in quarantine. I recognized them both immediately because their pictures had been on the front pages of newspapers for months. The number of men in quarantine at any one time is small, usually from twenty to fifty. They eat together, go together to the recreation yard, which is separated from the rest of the institution, and they have a lot of contact with one another.

I don't know what I expected when circumstances brought me together with David Greenglass for the first time and we started a conversation. I knew that this man, at that time, probably had one of the most infamous names in the world. To many he was a heartless being, a sub-human, because he was the prime witness against his sister, and it was his testimony that had put her in the electric chair. To many others he represented the highest form of treason, since he had stolen the atomic secrets and sold them to Russia. To Jews he held a unique status. He brought shame to the Jewish people and to many, fear of how his act might harm, in one way or another, Jews all over the world.

This was 1951. Israel had been in existence for only three years. The Korean War was in full steam, with American men fighting Communists and dying far from home. Senator Joseph McCarthy was at the peak of his power and influence. It has been true throughout Jewish history that when an individual Jew has committed an act of notoriety or shame, or has been accused of committing a notorious or shameful act, Jews collectively have been made to suffer in retaliation through acts of violence or repression directed against them. The famous Dreyfus case in France is but one example. When a Jew or Jews in the public eye do something disgraceful or criminal, it concerns other Jews wherever they may be. It follows, therefore, that when David came to Lewisburg, all the other Jews, who never numbered more than twenty or so out of a total prison population of about fifteen hundred, were emotionally and psychologically shaken.

In my initial discussions with David, I have to admit that I was fascinated by the situation. Here was a man who had done such terrible things, whose name and face were recognized throughout the world, and I was having small talk with him. As with most people, I had preconceived ideas of what to expect when meeting a famous or infamous person. It is easy to forget that the celebrity is only another human being, composed of both good and bad, and as the late Knute Rockne said, "They put their pants on one leg at a time."

David was a very likable person in many ways and he wanted to make friends. The more I got to know him, the more obvious it became that he had no real conception of the magnitude of his infamy and did not understand why people should hate him. David was a very simple man, of simple needs. He felt, and he was very open about it, that he had done a very dumb thing by stealing the atomic secrets. He also felt that his testimony against his sister was the right thing to do, because in that way he helped the government in that case as well as its investigation of other espionage cases. David had a childlike sense of humor. He would often giggle. He took pleasure in everything – it was as if he didn't realize that he was in a prison. He liked to eat. While most of us complained about the food, he didn't. He enjoyed eating. He took pleasure in his work. The job assigned to him was that of draftsman, and that was the kind of work he had done before coming to Lewisburg. He enjoyed the mechanical drawings that he did. He enjoyed the visits from the F.B.I., which occurred frequently, because the visits broke up the routine of the day. He didn't seem to have any fear of the future. He knew that upon the completion of his sentence, the government would give him a new identity. He would have a new name, a new area of the country to live in, and he not only hoped, he totally expected, to live a full and happy life the rest of his days after his release... and he probably has.

    David's impact on the general population of Lewisburg was not as great as the public would assume. There were many other famous and infamous men doing time during the same period. Initially, when he arrived, security was very strong and there was great concern for his safety. As time went on, his presence became relatively routine. Among the Jewish inmates, it took much longer for his presence to become routine. And even then, since there was a constant change in the make-up of the Jewish population with new inmates coming in and old ones leaving, the newly arrived Jewish inmates, without exception, didn't feel comfortable with him and couldn't act naturally in his presence.

Being an inmate in a federal penitentiary is difficult for anyone in terms of survival. Being Jewish in prison is ten times more difficult. Having a man with David Greenglass' past in our group was a constant source of concern for us. The Nazis, the lunatic fringe, and similar groups at Lewisburg did not make a distinction between David and the other Jewish inmates. He was a Jew and he was in close association with the other Jews in our group. As a Jew, he was entitled to come to Jewish services. And yet each person felt mixed emotions about having contact with him. Not only did he make the life of every other Jewish inmate more difficult, and possibly more dangerous, but he made each of us feel very uneasy about our own personal thoughts.

The more I got to know David during his first several months, the less I thought about what he had done. His crimes were not forgotten, but an inmate learns never to judge others. Everyone in prison has committed some crime. You learn that you judge each man as to how he conducts himself there, not for what he did in the past.

David was like a child in many ways. Most

things that would bother other men didn't bother him. Harry Gold, his colleague in espionage, told me a story that illustrated perfectly the type of man that David was. Harry had traveled across the United States from Philadelphia to New Mexico to meet David. He had taken a devious route, driving automobiles and riding on buses and trains, all the while making sure that he was not being followed. He had a date with destiny in Los Alamos, where he was to meet David Greenglass, who would turn over to him the secrets of the atomic bomb. Harry had rented a motel at a prearranged place. The time and date of the meeting had also been prearranged with David. As the rendezvous hour drew closer, Harry told me that he waited in extreme nervousness. He knew what he was doing. He knew the seriousness of his crime. As the moment drew near for David to knock on his door, he felt the tension mounting. Harry waited and waited... and waited. He was going crazy trying to guess what could possibly have delayed David. Had the F.B.I. found him out? Had he changed his mind? At a time like that a million thoughts cross your mind, and of the million possibilities that could have caused the delay of David Greenglass, Harry never dreamed of the real reason.

When David finally arrived, one hour late, Harry pulled him into the room and asked, "What happened?"

As Harry related the story to me, David was smiling and unconcerned. He said, "Nothing, Harry."

Harry said, "You're an hour late."

David smiled again, and said, "Yes, I know. I decided to go to the movies."

And that is a nutshell description of David Greenglass. Whether he was stealing the atomic secrets or serving his sentence in a federal penitentiary, he took nothing seriously and nothing bothered him.

David had a body that is best described as pear-shaped. He had a fat face. Much of his excess fat disappeared after his first year in prison, but he still kept his fat look. He smiled at inappropriate times. He was a man who, even before you got to know him, smacked of being shallow. Yet he was likeable. He seemed to feel no shame or responsibility for any of his criminal acts or for the death of his sister.

Over a period of years, David and I had many, many conversations about the exact details of how and why he got involved in espionage and what the circumstances were of his cooperation with the Government. He was the person who actually stole the atomic drawings. He did this, not by stealing the blueprints, as we have seen spies do in the movies so often. He memorized the drawings. David was probably in his middle twenties at the time this happened. He was a sergeant in the Army. He was able to examine the intricate plans for the atomic bomb and then go back to his apartment and make the drawings; look at the plans again and add to the drawings; and in this way he completed one of the most complex type of plans the world has ever known. These were the plans he passed on to Harry Gold, who passed them on to others. The surprising thing about David was that he wasn't the least bit embarrassed to discuss what had happened. David lacked something. He lacked the sensitivity of knowing what was right and what was wrong.

David did very easy time in prison in comparison to Harry Gold, who carried the weight of his crime heavily. I am quite sure that the general public could not conceive of the fact that with the burdens of his past David could be as lighthearted as he was most of the time. His explanation of why he testified against his sister and brother-in-law was very simple. He explained it very matter-of-factly. His explanation, in his eyes, eliminated all moral responsibility for his sister's death. He made a deal with the Government that he would cooperate and give them all the information he had. He would testify against his sister or anyone else they wanted him to testify against. For this they would release his wife, Ruth, from prosecution and would give him a reduced sentence (of fifteen years). It was understood by David that with his cooperation he would probably make parole in five years. His feeling was that his sister, Ethel, and brother-in-law Julius, had the same opportunity to cooperate with the American government, and they both chose not to. They were dedicated Soviet agents. He felt that they paid with their lives because that was their choice. According to David, even up until the last few days of their lives, U.S. government officials requesting cooperation and information concerning the espionage ring approached the Rosenbergs constantly. In return for their cooperation, their death sentences would be commuted. David felt grief at the death of his sister, but no responsibility.

The sentencing judge was Irving Kaufman, who later became Chief Judge of the U.S. Court of Appeals in New York.

Much has been written about the problems of security involving David Greenglass at Lewisburg. Being known as an informer for the F.B.I. places an inmate in a very bad position in any prison. To testify against a sister and cause her to die in the electric chair puts him in a position quite apart from all other hated men. The authorities at Lewisburg were in a quandary as to how to handle David. If he were killed or severely hurt, it wouldn't speak very well for the government's ability to protect its informers. If he were kept in isolation, an extremely difficult existence would be imposed on him, considering the length of his sentence. I feel that his situation was handled very well. He was assigned to a job as a mechanical draftsman in the inner office of the chief of mechanical services, where he was protected during his working hours. During his first three and a half years he remained in his cell after work. At least two days prior to and several days after the execution of his sister and brother-in-law, for his protection he was kept in his cell under total supervision. He did not leave even to go to his job. The authorities felt that if anyone meant to harm him, this was the time something would happen.

As head of the Jewish congregation, my duty was not to judge the severity of any crime of my fellow Jewish inmates, but to assist each one the best way I could. David was a likeable person. He had a beautiful sense of humor. He was a good conversationalist. He was appreciative of any kindness that was shown to him. He was intelligent, well read and knowledgeable in Judaism. I determined that I would treat him no differently than any other Jewish inmate.

One day, when I was in his place of work at the chief of mechanical services inner office, I said to him, "David, do you think you'll ever go out to the yard? You look terrible. Your skin looks like chalk. You haven't been out in the fresh air or sunshine for three and a half years."

He looked at me and asked, "Do you think it's safe?"

I answered, "I don't know, that decision is up to you."

He thought for a long time, looked at me with pleading in his eyes, and asked, "If I go, will you stay with me while I'm out there?"

I couldn't say no. I said, "O.K. David. Tomorrow after chow come out and I will meet you at the gate. Don't come out until everybody else is out. You be the last."

I didn't know what I had gotten myself into, but I had made a decision and given a promise. I decided to have my co-defendant, Demetrius, with me when David came out. Demetrius worked in the hospital as an assistant to the surgeon. This may not seem like a strong reason for having him with me, but it was. In Lewisburg, everyone is afraid that he will be cut up by another inmate for one reason or another. They want and they need a friend to be on the spot when they are being sewn up. Very few inmates ever did anything to offend Demetrius. I thought it would be an excellent idea to have him at my side when I walked around the exercise yard with David Greenglass on his first venture away from the safety of his office or cell.

When David came out to the yard, he was shaking like a leaf. I said, "David, just walk with me. Keep your mouth shut no matter what anybody says to you, and when I tell you to run, you get the hell out of there. If something goes wrong, you run as fast as your fat ass will take you."

As I had anticipated, everything went off without incident. Since everyone knew who he was and yet no one knew in advance that he was coming out that day, a stillness developed throughout the yard, and it was very quiet. We were out just a short while when I told David, "That's enough for today. Go on in."

The following day when he came out, he had so much confidence and was so natural as to appear to have almost forgotten the drama of the preceding day and how terribly frightened he was. Within a few days after that he would come out into the yard alone. He didn't need me anymore. He talked to different people, he walked, and he behaved like an ordinary inmate. David didn't understand that the main reason nothing unpleasant happened was not because he was well liked, and not because the inmates didn't know who he was, and not because no one cared. It was a matter of simple inmate self-preservation and their understanding of prison procedures. They knew that David was being watched through binoculars by perhaps ten guards posted in doors and windows and that if anyone attempted to harm him the guards would spot it in a second. They would probably stop any incident before it happened, and they would certainly grab the inmate who was going to do him harm. He would be immediately shipped off to Alcatraz and any chance for future parole would be killed.

This was the basic nature of David. He was not a worrier. He was childlike in many ways. He would discuss the most sensitive and delicate of subjects with total unconcern. He had been convicted of one of the most heinous crimes in American history and yet he felt no burden about it. As time passed, he even refused to believe that his fellow inmates hated him.

There is one story that David told me, which probably has never been in print before. The story involved his wife Ruth. I always felt that David loved his wife and children very dearly. I think whatever grief he felt about his sister's death totally vanished when he saw his wife in the visiting room, knowing that because of him she was a free woman and able to take care of their children. David told me that the F.B.I. had given his wife a new identity, a change of name, all proper identification papers, and educational verification. With this new identity she went out job hunting. She was a very able woman and, obviously, had as much chutzpah as her husband. Of all the jobs in the world open to her, she wound up as personal secretary to the Canadian Ambassador to the United Nations. I heard this story one day from David when he had just returned from the visiting room, talking to his wife Ruth. He was so bubbling over with laughter and good humor that his stomach was bouncing up and down.

He said, "I've got to tell you the funniest story you've ever heard in your life."

Then he explained to me about Ruth getting a new identity and securing a job with the Canadian Ambassador to the U.N. He told me that she had worked there for several months until, by chance, one of the Assistant United States Attorneys handling the espionage trial came into her office and saw her. As David told the story, the Assistant U.S. Attorney rushed in to see the Ambassador and asked him, "Do you know who you have working for you?"

Of course, the Canadian Ambassador couldn't believe the story he was told. He explained to the Assistant U.S. Attorney that the Canadian government and the United Nations run a very thorough security check on all personnel, and most particularly on any assistants he might have. What the Ambassador didn't realize was that the F.B.I. had been so very competent and thorough in giving Ruth Greenglass a new identity that the U.N. security people were not able to penetrate her cover. This was an example of David Greenglass' sense of humor. He thought it was a very, very funny story.

FOUR CRISES

During my five years, three months, and twenty-seven days in prison I constantly walked a tightrope to maintain a proper relationship with both the inmates and the officials. On awakening each morning I faced the unpredictable, savage atmosphere of prison life. An inmate learns to be very cunning and observant in order to survive. Some will find survival easier than others. I had many near brushes with calamity, but there were four times during my prison existence that I consider the most critical.

The first occurred when I had been in Lewisburg only a short time. During that period I deliberately had as little contact with the other inmates as possible. One night, after lights out, I was lying in my bunk with my eyes open, unable to sleep. This is almost a universal problem with inmates. I saw a large man sneaking down the aisle between the bunks. I recognized him immediately. He was an uneducated military prisoner. I had observed him in the past and I knew that he was a very rough, crude person. I didn't know anything else about him and had never spoken with him. As he came sneaking down the aisle, I didn't watch him because I didn't care what he was up to and I didn't want him to know that I was aware of him, so I looked straight ahead. To my great shock, he stopped at my bunk and stooped down to almost a crouch. He stood there, crouched, and looked straight at me. An inmate knows that anything is possible in prison and he learns to think quickly. I determined that my best move was to say nothing and do nothing... just keep my eyes open, look straight ahead, but watch him from the side of my eyes at all times. What was in his mind, I didn't know. He nay have come there for sex; he may have come there to knife me; he may have come there to beat me with his fists; and very possibly he may have come there just for his own personal excitement to frighten me. There is no way of knowing how much time went by. He stood in his crouched position, very close to my face, staring directly at me. This became a test of strength between two men. I didn't know what he wanted or what he would do. If I said anything, or made any move, this would eliminate all of the question marks. He could then have proceeded to try to do whatever was in his mind. I felt the vibrations between us and knew that the longer he waited the less confident he felt about his position. Initially, he was the aggressor and I was on the defensive. As time went on, our positions equalized, and I felt the fear in his heart as to when I would make my move, and how. I really don't know whether I was afraid or not. My job was survival, and through luck or strength, I survived. After awhile, he got up and walked down the aisle towards his own bunk. I saw this man on many occasions during the years after this incident. I never spoke of it nor did he. There is no way of my knowing what it was all about.

There was an inmate named Sahm, who was an interesting study. He had been in and out of prisons most of his life. He took great pleasure in being involved in any illegal scheme in the prison that he thought would give him an opportunity to outwit or outsmart the officials. He took great glee in tormenting any inmate he felt would not retaliate. It seemed that his only purpose in life was to make his fellow prisoners do harder time and suffer to the maximum. He loved the intrigue of extorting money from some of the older and wealthier inmates. He offered them protection from other inmates, whose threats he had originally instigated, or he threatened them himself. The family of the threatened inmate would be required to send sums of money to contacts of Sahm on the outside. More often than not, his tormenting of the other men was solely for the purpose of his evil gratification and not for any monetary gain. On various occasions during my time in Lewisburg he had created difficulties for me, which I was able to handle in one way or another so that no serious consequences developed. I knew that by the nature of the man that he would continue to persist. It was a game that stimulated him.

My constant objective was to maintain a good record and to make parole at the earliest possible moment. It was after a set of circumstances that he had set up involving other inmates that caused me greater problems than ever before, that I finally made a very serious and important decision. I said to myself, "I cannot avoid this man anymore. I must have a head to head meeting and a definite understanding between us."

It took me a long time – several months – to make this decision. One day I approached Sahm's cell and told him that I would like to talk with him.

He was surprised at seeing me, but he said, "Come on in."

I stood and looked at him for a few moments before I spoke. I finally said, "Sahm, you've known me for a long time. You know and I know that you've created a lot of problems for me. You've given me a lot of shit and I've taken it. There is only one reason that I have, and I want you to know what that reason is. I am a first offender and I'll probably make parole. That's the most important fact of my life here. I have taken shit from you because I don't want any trouble. If I get into something with you I'm going to go into the hole. And that will hurt my chance of parole. Now, you know me pretty well, Sahm. You see that I'm not emotional right now. You see that I'm very calm. I'm very serious and I mean every word that I say. I will continue to take shit from you and to put up with the Goddamn problems you cause me because I don't want any trouble. However, I want it understood between us right now that if, because of you, even though I try to avoid trouble, it becomes unavoidable and you cause me to lose parole, I will kill you. Do we understand each other?"

He didn't say a word, but from that day on, I

never had any troubles with Sahm.

There was an inmate who worked in the electrical shop whose name was Jones. He was a very mean person. He never smiled, never laughed, and never had anything good to say about anything. As a matter of fact, he didn't talk much, period. Most inmates were wary of him. He was cruel and he was known to carry a shank. A shank is a homemade knife made of a piece of metal. Jones was involved in many illicit activities in prison. We had very little contact with each other over the years until one day I was in my cell with my back to the door, washing my face, when Jones suddenly opened the door and rushed in. No one ever opens another man's cell without asking permission first. I knew his reputation and the fact that we were not on friendly terms made me realize immediately that at any second he might pull a knife and attack me. A man learns to react with jungle cat quickness within the prison walls. Had I made any sudden moves I might have been dead in a matter of seconds. When I heard the door open, I looked in the mirror in front of me where I was washing my face and I saw who had entered.

In a calm, firm voice I said, "Hello, Jones."

I could see that he was getting very nervous at this point. He didn't know what to expect from me and he knew that by being in my cell he was violating a very strong unwritten rule among inmates.

In a very agitated voice he said, "I found out you've been ratting on me."

I calmly looked him in the eyes and said, "Jones, you know that's not true. You know my reputation. You know I have been clean for a long time. And another thing – I could have put the finger on you two years ago for smuggling those chickens out of the kitchen in the stoves that you repair. Don't you think that I've known that every time you bring a stove up from the kitchen for repair you've got at least two or three chickens in there? Hell, everybody in the electric shop knows you've been stealing chickens." I said, "You know I'm not dumb. I could have had you buried a long time ago if I wanted to. Nobody ever found out about those chickens, did they, Jones? You brought some up today. Now, whoever told you about me made a mistake. Let's forget the whole thing."

He hung his head and said, "O.K." and he left

my cell.

After I had officially been notified that I had made parole and I had less than two months to serve before release, a most sensitive and delicate situation took place in the mess hall. As much as a man attempts to maintain a good record and to keep out of trouble during his sentence, he tries doubly hard once he has made parole. If he gets involved in any type of disciplinary action between the granting of parole and his release, the parole will be rescinded.

It was lunchtime in the mess hall, and there were between twelve and fifteen hundred men eating there. A waiter, who was carrying a container of water to my table, approached me and pointed at me, and someone several tables down nodded.

The waiter said, "The Chief wants me to give you a message. He's going to cut your throat." He said it loud enough so that all the inmates for several tables around heard.

I told the waiter, "You're making a mistake. You better find out whom you're supposed to give that message to. It's not for me."

Again, he looked down several rows of tables,

pointed at me, and the other inmate nodded his head. The waiter said, "There's no mistake. You're the man the Chief wants me to give the message to."

Obviously, even a person who has never been in prison can see that the next development could be a matter of life and death. An inmate learns to think quickly and to know his adversary. I knew that this Chief he spoke of was an American Indian who was serving time in Lewisburg for a murder conviction on an Indian reservation. I knew that if I showed weakness in front of the other men I would be inviting the same sort of treatment from all of them for the remainder of my sentence. I would also be inviting the Chief to carry out his threat. He was already serving life for murder. He had been in trouble constantly and he had no hope of parole. The one thing of importance to him in Lewisburg was his reputation as a tough guy. On the other hand, if I challenged him openly in the mess hall within earshot of all his cohorts, he would have no alternative but to carry out his threat in order to preserve his image.

I told the waiter, and I spoke loud enough so that everyone would hear, "You tell the Chief that I received his message and I'll meet him in front of our cellblock right after chow." Everything became very quiet in the mess hall. No one knew what to expect, but everyone expected that there would be blood shed.

I knew that because of the seating arrangement I would be at the cellblock first. He would have a lot of time to wonder what I was going to do while he approached me. I also knew that all the inmates would disperse and leave him alone because he was not liked, and no one wanted to get involved. He didn't know what I had in my mind, but I knew what was in his mind. That gave me an advantage. He probably assumed that I would be standing inside the cellblock waiting for him to arrive. I did the opposite. I stood exactly where the main hallway enters the cellblock so that we were in view of everyone. As he approached me, I watched him walking towards me, and he watched me watching and waiting for him. I felt that I had the psychological advantage.

As he came within hearing distance of me I spoke calmly and softly. I said, "Let's talk, Chief."

He stood perhaps six feet from me because he

was a very astute fighter. He didn't want to get too close until he was ready.

I said, "Chief, you've made a mistake."

He said, "I didn't make a mistake."

I said, "We don't know each other very well, but we've seen each other around a long time. Why?"

He said, "Because you've been playing around with my girlfriend."

I said, "Who told you that?" He told me another inmate's name that was a known homosexual.

I said, "That's not true, chief. You know I don't go that way. Your girlfriend came to my shop two or three times carrying a message. We had no other contact than that, and anybody who told you different is setting you up." I said, "Now look, Chief. We both know our way around this joint. That's a bad thing you said in the mess hall. I figure you made a mistake and I'm willing to forget it. You want to forget it?"

"O.K." he said.

And that was the end.

ALGER HISS

The name of Alger Hiss has probably become one of the most famous names in American criminal history. This man had nothing to do with the fall of Richard Nixon, but he certainly was extremely instrumental in the rise of Richard Nixon.

In the fifties, in Lewisburg, many of the left wing and Communist inmates had been put there because of Senator Joseph McCarthy of Wisconsin. In the case of Alger Hiss, his imprisonment was due to a young and obscure congressman from California by the name of Richard Milhous Nixon. On the strength of the congressional hearings that sent Alger Hiss to Lewisburg, Nixon was elected to the United States Senate, and went on to become Vice President, and subsequently was elected to the Presidency. During Alger Hiss' period of incarceration at Lewisburg, Richard Nixon became Vice President of the United States. Of all the crimes that Nixon had accused Hiss of, the only conviction against him was for perjury. His perjury was in connection with damaging documents found hidden in a pumpkin, which became known worldwide as the "Pumpkin Papers." Whitaker Chambers, a self-avowed former Communist, was the primary witness against Hiss. Opinion was divided then – and still is – as to who told the truth, Hiss or Chambers.

Alger Hiss was a frail man, taller than six feet. He had risen to international fame with the State Department, peaked by his introductory message at the opening session of the United Nations in San Francisco in 1945. He had seen his fame turn to infamy under the inquisition of Richard Nixon. He was determined to survive physically in the jungle in which he found himself. His method of survival was to surround himself with the tough New York Italian group. It was obvious to anyone with any common sense that he didn't choose his companions for their intellectual compatibility, but his chosen colleagues felt honored at having a man of his stature and fame discuss world affairs with them. They offered to protect him, which protection he received throughout his stay in Lewisburg. He made a determined effort not to make friends or enemies. When he was not alone, he was in the company of the Italian group.

He was totally cautious in his conduct because he wanted to antagonize no one. Even the convicted acknowledged Communists did not receive a cold shoulder from Hiss. Douglas Chandler, a Nazi convicted of treason and serving life, was greeted respectfully and they engaged in cordial conversation. The men he spent most of his time with were of a low educational level and someone of Hiss' past experience and education must have sorely missed the intellectual stimulation he was accustomed to. He was liked very much by all the uneducated and economically deprived inmates because they felt most honored to be in his company. He insisted that everyone call him "Al." Among the higher educated inmates, Alger Hiss was generally held somewhat in contempt because the reasons for his exclusive association with his chosen friends were obvious. We all felt that it was his privilege to choose his own method of survival during his sentence. However, it was also felt that his method was not very admirable. He was in complete bondage to men who could give him only one thing to ease the burden of his prison years – freedom from fear of physical harm – and he must have suffered more than anyone can imagine.

    Due to the political climate of McCarthyism in America in the middle 1950's, left wing or Communist prisoners, regardless of their educational abilities, were not utilized in the education department, although Nazis were. Douglas Chandler was a teacher. Al was given an obscure job that combined minor clerical work with physical loading and unloading. His job title was clerk in the supply department. His department handled supplies of every type needed to run the institution except foodstuffs, which came under another department. His job required very little ability and frequently very little activity. For a man who must have carried enormous emotional and psychological burdens, this was perhaps one of the worst types of jobs. He had too much time to think. Perhaps this was the very reason he was assigned to that particular job. Let us not forget that he was Richard Nixon's claim to fame, and Richard Nixon was then Vice President of the United States. Al would have made a perfect teacher. There were basic subjects that he could have taught to the many, many men in Lewisburg who were practically illiterate. He would have had large classes with waiting lists because it would have been a source of pride and something an inmate could talk about for the rest of his life – that Alger Hiss had been his teacher.

Alger Hiss was a man who never spoke without great care in the choice of every word and caution as to what meaning his statement could have to the different ears that might be listening. He would never speak in specifics, only in generalities. The simplest, most unimportant questions would be answered with the utmost deliberation. The time span between his thoughts and his words was so lengthy as to be annoying. We had a standard joke about Al in Lewisburg. If you asked him what time it was, between the time he thought over the question and decided just how to formulate his answer, it was already too late, and you no longer wanted to know. It was impossible to really get to know this man. In prison, most men let their hair down and you can learn what makes them tick – you can get to know the real person behind the façade. I took pride in sizing up inmates and making life and death decisions on my judgments. But not with Al – he was like a stick of wood. He rarely laughed and never, but never, showed anger. He was always in total control of himself. His personality behind the walls was heavy bland. I have always wondered if this was a prison affectation or if this was the real Alger Hiss.

As cool and collected as Al seemed to be during his stay in Lewisburg, there was one thing that occurred when he first entered Lewisburg that proved to me that he was not always as calm, deliberate, and controlled as he appeared. Everyone entering Lewisburg received educational, psychological, and medical testing. The results of these tests were utilized to determine the type of jobs assigned to the inmates. Since Alger Hiss was a household name to all the inmates and custodial staff and his intellectual achievements had been written up frequently in the newspapers, everyone was very interested in hearing what score he had made on his educational tests. The scores on these tests are supposedly for the eyes only of the upper echelon officials. However, as with everything else in prison, the typing and handling is done by inmates. When inmates are involved in any procedure in prison, even confidential matters soon become general knowledge to the rest of the prison population. Alger Hiss' score was unbelievably low. No one assumed that he was a stupid man because of the score, but understood that he must have been in such psychological turmoil at the time of the testing that it was impossible for him to function properly.

Many of us had gone through the same experience. It is interesting that Al was so embarrassed by his low score that after he had adjusted himself to his prison situation, he requested of the officials and received permission to take the test a second time. Of course, he received an outstanding grade.

The one thing that brought Al and me close together was the Lewisburg debating team. For reasons of his own, he chose not to become a part of our group in any capacity. However, when I called upon him for assistance on a debate on which I was representing Lewisburg against a nearby college, he readily offered all his time and knowledge to help me. The subject of the debate was "Resolved that free trade be established in the United States between our country and foreign nations." This was a field in which Al was probably as knowledgeable as any living American.

His first suggestion to me was, "Read a book called 'The Wealth of Nations' by Adam Smith."

The library had the book and it was about three inches thick. It had been written perhaps two hundred years ago and was the basis for the growth of the British Empire. After reading the book I had a basic knowledge of what the debate was about, and from there Al assisted me in the more important thrusts of the pro and con.

There was one incident involving Al that the total population of Lewisburg witnessed with anticipation. It was the day William Remington was released from quarantine and entered the recreation area for the first time. Whether or not these two men had ever met personally previously, I have no way of knowing. But, obviously, each had read much about the other. As Bill Remington walked the recreation yard alone, as he would do many times in the future, Al approached him and put out his hand to shake. Bill Remington declined the offer of Al's hand, nodded to him, and walked on. No one will ever know what was said between these two men except Alger Hiss because not too many months later Bill Remington was brutally murdered in Lewisburg.

When Al's time in Lewisburg was up, the news media from all over the world was waiting at the front gate. His answers to the probing questions of the reporters were just as cautious and generalized as I had learned to expect from him.

DEMETRIUS

One of my many responsibilities as secretary in the electrical shop was handling the distribution and repair of earphones. In those days there were no television sets in prison, even though they were widely used on the outside. Each cell or bunk in a dormitory had an outlet where the inmate could plug in his earphones. There were two channels, A and B, which had radio programs selected by the officials, which they felt would be suitable. As new men arrived on the prison bus and were placed in quarantine, my office would be notified of the names and numbers of the newcomers so that earphones could be issued to them. The names of new arrivals and the names of men about to leave are top secret information in prison. The warden's office and the offices of the two associate wardens handled these tight security matters, but because of a quirk in the system, I received this information as soon as they did.

One day I received the list and routinely read through the names. I couldn't believe my eyes when I saw the name of Demetrius. It gave me a jolt because he had been the co-defendant in my case. Co-defendants are not usually sent to the same federal prison. To the best of my knowledge, Demetrius had been in Terre Haute, Indiana for the last three years. I immediately called the inmate working in the quarantine section and asked him if Demetrius had come from Terre Haute. He said, "Yes."

This was a moment of extreme emotion for me. I had made my life behind the walls without contact with anyone whom I had known on the outside or who knew anything about my past. Demetrius was more than a co-defendant. He had been a close personal friend for many years. Having a friend, a real friend, in prison is a rare experience.

Usually, the delivery of earphones to new inmates is not made until three or four days after arrival. In Demetrius' case I made sure that he had his within one hour after entering his cell. I found out later from him that he was the envy of everyone in his cellblock. Of course, no one, not even Demetrius, knew why he had received this favored treatment. The first night he spent in Lewisburg, Bobo Olson was fighting for the world's middleweight championship. Most inmates in prison probably expend eighty per cent of their conversation and thoughts on sporting events of one kind or another. Sports are a constant source of discussion, argument, and gambling. Because he had earphones to listen to the fight, Demetrius was the center of attention throughout the cellblock. After each round it was his duty to announce to all the other inmates within shouting distance what had happened.

Demetrius, of course, knew that I was at Lewisburg, or he assumed that I was still there. In the federal prison system, you never know who will be transferred and when, and for what reason. I secured a pass from the Protestant chaplain that would allow me to be present the next morning when the quarantined prisoners came into their separate mess hall for breakfast. Under normal circumstances I would not have been allowed there. However, most of the guards knew me and I had legal permission to be there, supposedly to speak with a Jewish inmate. I was not questioned. I spotted Demetrius, yelled at him, and grabbed his hand. He was as glad to see me as I was to see him, but since he had just come from another penitentiary he was well aware of the strict rules of quarantine. He was afraid that he would get in trouble with the officials on his first day and that I would certainly be punished. The meeting was very brief. I told Demetrius that I would be seeing him periodically.

Having been at Lewisburg for three years at this time, my position of influence was considerable, both among the inmates and the officials, and I knew my way around. I was aware that Demetrius was an intelligent man and in all likelihood could handle any job that was assigned to him. I determined to use my influence to get him the best type of job possible. Generally speaking, the hospital is one of the best places to work in any prison. You always have enough to eat. The inmates are issued white uniforms, which are kept clean, and the work is interesting. I was quite familiar with the selection committee procedures for the work assignment of new prisoners. I knew that the chief medical officer sat on this committee. His inmate secretary was a friend of mine for whom I had done many favors. I went to the hospital to see him that same day and I informed him that my rap partner, prison jargon for co-defendant, had just arrived from Terre Haute. I told him that he was a very intelligent guy and would be an asset to the hospital. I asked him as a favor to me, to mention to his boss, the chief medical officer, that a good man had just arrived from Terre Haute and should be selected to work in the hospital. The chief medical officer was always on the lookout for someone of ability to add to his hospital staff. Most of the men in prison are not very reliable or diligent and there is a constant change of hospital personnel. It makes the operation of the hospital much easier if they get a good man upon arrival and teach him a specific job.

Of course, I convinced my inmate friend that Demetrius was very qualified and that I wanted him in the hospital as a favor to me. He owed me and couldn't say no. No doubt, when he spoke to the chief medical officer, he exaggerated Demetrius' qualifications quite a bit in order to swing the deal. Since Demetrius was a transfer from another federal institution, he was not required to stay the full thirty days in quarantine. Within a few days he was released to general population, given a dormitory, and assigned to work in the hospital. When I had asked my friend to have Demetrius assigned to the hospital, I didn't request a specific job because I was aware that many of the jobs in the hospital required technical training and frequently there were no openings for the best jobs. To my complete surprise, Demetrius was assigned to the operating room as an assistant in surgery. I contacted my friend, the chief medical officer's secretary, and asked him why Demetrius had been assigned to the operating room.

His answer was very simple. "You wanted him to have a good job. I gave him one of the best jobs in the hospital."

Whether Demetrius was qualified to handle this or not, whether he had the stomach for it or not, whether he could be properly trained for it or not, didn't seem to matter. If he could handle the job, fine. If he couldn't, he would be out. My friend felt that he had totally fulfilled his end of the bargain.

In our pre-prison days, Demetrius was ten pounds lighter than I was in weight. I weighed 175 pounds and he weighed 165 pounds. When he arrived in Lewisburg, he was fifteen pounds heavier than when I had known him. He weighed 180 pounds. I was fifteen pounds lighter than when he had last seen me. I weighed 160 pounds. We were both shocked at the change in each other's appearance. The reason for the shift in weight was the subject of a long conversation between us and we determined the reasons. I have always been very particular about the food I ate, and the prison fare frequently was so objectionable to me that I couldn't eat it. Also, I was a heavy smoker and the twelve dollar limitation on spending at the commissary barely covered my purchases of cigarettes and other personal necessities. I had no money left over for candies or cookies. Demetrius, on the other hand, had always eaten any kind of food, and whether or not the prison food was pleasurable, he ate heartily of whatever was served. His first job in Terre Haute was as a worker in the bakery and he ate part of everything he baked for the several months he was there. In addition, he had stopped smoking when he arrived at Terre Haute, and instead of spending his twelve dollars on cigarettes as I did, he was able to use his money to buy all kinds of goodies. Because he ate all the food he was served in the mess hall, his bakery extras, and all the goodies he bought in the commissary, Demetrius started getting fat. He determined to be very active in sports to work his new fat into muscle. He chose weight lifting as his sport. Any weight lifter knows that weight lifting does not trim you down and eliminate fat; it develops muscles out of the fat.

When I saw Demetrius, even though he was fifteen pounds heavier, there wasn't an ounce of fat on him. He was one solid walking muscle. We stayed together in Lewisburg for two years and were eventually released on the same day. At the time of release, Demetrius had lost fifteen pounds from the weight he carried at the time he came to Lewisburg and I had gained fifteen pounds. The explanation is interesting. Since he didn't smoke, we could use all of his twelve dollars for candy bars and cookies. He spent every nickel, and half the goodies went to me. Immediately, within a couple of weeks, I started to put on weight and gradually, month after month, my weight increased. Demetrius' situation was the opposite. Because he didn't have as many goodies to eat as he had before, his weight started to decrease. Also, instead of only lifting weights for exercise, he and I would play handball at every available opportunity.

Fortunately, for all concerned, Demetrius liked his job assignment in the operating room very much. He had a natural aptitude, of which I had not been aware, and he quickly learned the procedures from the surgeon and the number one inmate assistant. It was during his first month in the operating room that he asked the chief surgeon why there was no clock in the operating room. The surgeon explained that he had been requesting a clock in the operating room for several years but, due to budgetary problems, there was always more important equipment that the hospital needed and acquisition of a clock had always been denied by the purchasing officials.

Demetrius told him, "I'll get you a clock."

The surgeon looked at him in surprise and said, "How can you get me a clock?"

Demetrius told him, "Doctor, don't worry about it. If you want a clock, I'll get it for you. I don't know how soon I will be able to get it, but you'll get a clock."

Demetrius explained the situation to me. He said, "You've got to get me a clock."

I said, "Jesus Christ, Demetrius, that's a

tough request. Clocks are hard to come by."

He said, "Can you do it?"

I said, "Give me a couple of days."

This was going to be a problem. Good electric clocks were always in demand by the top officials and the few that were available in the supply room were guarded like Fort Knox. Acquisition of a clock for Demetrius would require all the abilities and experience I could draw upon. I went to see Alger Hiss, who was the clerk in the supply department. I asked him which offices in Lewisburg got a clock upon request.

He said, "Hell, that's one of the most difficult things to get out of the supply room." He added, "The warden has to approve that."

My mind got busy and I hatched a plot. I sent over one of my inmate electricians to the warden's office. I had called in advance to tell the warden's secretary that the inmate was coming to do the usual annual maintenance on the clock. I told my inmate worker that he was to take the clock down, pretend to be oiling it, and then inform the warden's secretary that there was a part broken and the clock would have to be taken back to the shop for replacement of the part. As soon as my worker brought me the clock, I called the warden's secretary. I told him that I was very sorry to report that the broken part in the clock could not be replaced. The warden's secretary raised hell and demanded that I get a clock up there immediately. I explained that I would be very happy to if he would write out a requisition for a new clock from the storeroom and have the warden sign it. I myself went to the warden's office to pick up the requisition slip that had been signed by the warden and took it down to the supply room. When the officer in charge saw the warden's signature, he immediately gave me a new clock. My worker inmate took the new clock to the warden's office and installed it. Then the two of us, my inmate worker and I, went to the operating room in the hospital.

    I said, "Demetrius, tell me where you want it."

    This whole scenario had taken less than twenty-four hours from the time Demetrius had first asked for the clock. I left immediately after the clock was installed because I wanted no more part of this situation.

When the surgeon came into the operating room, Demetrius pointed to the clock and said, "How do you like it, doctor? Is it in the right place?"

The doctor was flabbergasted. He said, "Where did you get it?"

Demetrius said, "You promised not to ask, doctor." To this day, that same clock is probably in the operating room in Lewisburg.

Now that Demetrius was secure in his job, my next effort was to get proper living quarters for him. It took me two years to work my way up from dormitory to semi-honor dormitory to honor cellblock. As a personal favor to me, the associate warden's secretary, through methods of his own which I never questioned, had Demetrius in semi-honor within a month and two months after that he was three cells away from me in "J" block, the honor cellblock.

"IT WAS LIKE A MAGNET DREW ME"

In prison men do many illogical and unpredictable things. It goes with the territory. I knew a man who had been transferred to the prison farm because of his good conduct and the fact that he was "getting short." I didn't know this man well, but well enough to know that he was mentally stable. He was only on the farm about two months when he attempted an escape and was caught. He had less than thirty days to go before release at the time of his attempted escape. The penalty for attempting an escape from a federal institution is a maximum sentence of five years. Most men who escape without harming anyone receive six months to a year's additional time. This inmate was brought back inside the walls and assigned to his prior job.

I asked him one day to explain something to me. I said, "I've known you for a couple of years. You're an intelligent guy. You're very stable. Why did you try an escape when you only had thirty days left?"

His answer was very intriguing. He said. "I

don't know. I didn't want to go to the farm. I had a very odd feeling about going outside the walls where I could escape if I wanted to. Every night I couldn't sleep. I was going crazy. Inside the walls you have no choice. On the farm, freedom is available. I couldn't help myself. It was like a magnet drew me. There were no plans made. I just jumped up in the middle of the night and started running. I just couldn't help it."

TO GRAPPLE WITH AN APPLE

On my first trip outside the prison walls with my boss, Mr. Walters, I was in a state of childlike fear. My chief concern was that if I got too far away from my boss some officer might think I was trying to escape or was doing something that I wasn't supposed to do. It was so important for my record to be given medium custody and go outside the walls that I was petrified at the thought that any misunderstanding might develop whereby this privilege would be rescinded. Mr. Walters understood my fear because he had witnessed it many times before in other men.

During the latter part of our first day he had to visit someone in an office and left me in the truck alone. When he came back he handed me an apple. I asked, "What's this, Mr. Walters?"

He said, "Damn, haven't you ever seen an apple before?"

I said, "Why are you giving it to me?"

He said, "Don't you want to eat it?"

I said, "Mr. Walters, I don't want to do anything that's going to get me in trouble or get you in trouble."

He said, "You're with me. You're not going to get in any trouble when you're with me."

I said, "I appreciate it very much, but I'm afraid."

He said, "Look, there's something in the back of the truck I want you to get for me. Go back in there and take that damn apple with you."

I went to the back of the truck and I ate my apple. I don't think I enjoyed it very much because when you live under extreme regimentation and you have such a fear of violating the rules because of the effect the violation might have on your early release, you develop a conditioned reflex. It takes a long time to develop this habit of prison obedience, and it also takes a long time to regain your independence of action.

BILL REMINGTON

Bill Remington was a man who didn't receive as much publicity as Alger Hiss, but in the web of McCarthyism that prevailed at that time, his case was as important. He was considered one of America's leading experts on the economy, was a graduate of Dartmouth University, and at the time of his conviction he was a very high official in the United States Department of Commerce. He was a very handsome man, in his early thirties, at least six feet two, and in excellent physical condition. His only crime was to be convicted of perjury before a United States Senate Committee. He had stated under oath before the committee that "I am not now nor have I ever been a member of the Communist Party." He was unlucky enough to have a bitter ex-wife who was happy to testify in front of the Senate that he had, indeed, been a member of the Young Communist League when she dated him at Dartmouth. Afterwards, he admitted this, but he claimed that he had only been a member for about two weeks. He was a member at the beginning of World War II, when many liberals were pro-Russian as well as anti-Nazi, and he was about nineteen years old at the time.

In contrast to the many left wing prisoners in Lewisburg, Bill showed no sympathy for the liberal movement. His one purpose in life was to convince the American government and the American people that he was a patriotic American. Many of the other men, including Alger Hiss, denied any criminal guilt in their activities. But they were very proud of their liberal sympathies and of the movements they had supported in their lifetimes. Bill Remington wanted no association whatsoever with any of the left wing political prisoners. He constantly hoped for a new trial and he knew that the prison officials would be watching him closely as to his associates and activities.

Every inmate has his own method of physical survival in a prison. Most survive through the employment of distasteful, devious prison politics. Bill Remington was young, strong, handsome, and he looked like someone from the cover of *Sports Illustrated*. He determined that in the vermin-infested environment in which he was forced to live he wouldn't take any stuff from anybody. And he was big enough and strong enough to back up his determination.

Bill showed his individuality in many ways, but there is one particular small event that I have thought about many times. About twice a month spaghetti was served for dinner. This was a big event, not because the spaghetti was so tasty, but because this was one of the few meals when you could have as much as you wanted. The rule with spaghetti, as with anything else, was that you never left anything on your tray. I was sitting next to Bill and to my astonishment I saw that he took his spaghetti and made a sandwich with it. I had never seen a spaghetti sandwich before and I kidded him about it. The other inmates sitting nearby saw him eating the spaghetti sandwich and began to ridicule him. He ignored all comments and said, "I like to eat spaghetti in a sandwich." And that was the end of that.

Bill Remington was assigned to work in the hospital. Since he was on various shifts in the hospital, he had quite a bit of spare time to go outside to the athletic yard. Here he did two things. He ran the track and he played handball. I watched this man run the track and I have never in my life seen a more graceful runner. I learned that he had been on the track team at Dartmouth. You could see on his face, as he made his turns around the track, that his running was effortless and that he knew exactly what he was doing. I got to know Bill by playing handball. He was very selective in his friends. His conversations were generally just small talk. He had no desire to discuss his case or his personal life. He was a straightforward clean type of man who asked no favors and volunteered none. He required nothing of his fellow inmates or the authorities except to be left alone to do his time. This man, who had such great gifts of intellect, personality, physical stature, and looks, failed to realize one thing. He was in prison. His attributes in themselves offended most of the other prisoners because their inferiority to him was so obvious. And he made no pretense of attempting to make them feel more comfortable.

Bill Remington was murdered.

The media gave many reasons for his murder. The two most widely circulated theories were that he had been involved in homosexual activity or that some patriotic American in Lewisburg had killed him because of his Communist connections. Both of these reports were disgustingly erroneous. Bill Remington's job in the hospital at this particular time required that he work all night and, therefore, sleep in the daytime. He was in a cell with three other men. Someone decided to steal his cigarettes and he awoke and caught them in the act. He was beaten to death by blows to the head from a metal pipe. Brain surgery was performed in the operating room at Lewisburg. Had he survived, he would have been a jabbering idiot.

I was interrogated by the F.B.I. after this homicide. It was known that I played handball with Bill and the authorities had determined that he had very few other friends in the entire prison population. They assumed that I knew what had happened. I did not know until the facts came out afterwards. Bill Remington was horribly maligned in the press after his murder. Nowhere was the real story ever presented. I have seen many men murdered in prison and hundreds wounded, but none had the effect on me that Bill did. This superb human being, endowed by the gods with so many gifts, had been erased by scum. I have always felt certain that it was more than the cigarettes that caused the attack on Bill Remington. The men around him, by his bearing and attitude, were made too uncomfortably aware of their inferiority.

THE ELK THAT CAME TO DINNER

Eating time in prison is a very big event. It breaks the routine, and regardless of how humble or tasteless the food is it's food, and most of the time the inmates are hungry. There were always comedians who loved to spread false rumors about what we were going to have for any given meal. They pretended to have seen the food or had been told by friends in the mess hall. Everyone would become elated at the prospect of beef or chicken or ham with the excitement mounting as the rumor spread from building to building. As we entered the mess hall the smell that came out was unmistakable – Spanish rice. There were very few men who treated this bit of comedy with laughter. Some felt like crying and most, I am sure, would have liked to wring the neck of the man who had spread the false rumor.

There was one time, however, when even the biggest liar in the joint could not have made up a story as wild as the one that turned out to be the truth. The U.S. Department of the Interior had been plagued with an over-abundance of elk in our national parks. In order to protect the herds from starvation, they had to eliminate some of the elk population, which was growing too fast for the food supply. The U.S. Park officials started to slaughter these animals and they notified the Army, the Navy, the Air Force, the Coast Guard, and the U.S. Federal Bureau of Prisons that they had X number of pounds of elk to be distributed free. Each service was offered an allotment. Of course, rumors came to our ears of a great shipment of elk arriving in downtown Lewisburg, but no one believed these ridiculous stories. In truth, refrigerated cars did come in full of the elk from Yellowstone National Park and other national parks. We had no facilities to refrigerate such a large quantity of food and private commercial space was rented in the nearby city. For perhaps a month we ate like kings. We had elk steak, elk roast, elk stew, and elk dishes of every type and variety that the cooks could dream up. They gave us large quantities and it was very tasty. From that time onward, the practical jokers had a field day. No one knew what to believe or what to disbelieve because we knew that anything was possible.

THE BALLET OF THE LONG MOPS

The main corridor of Lewisburg is like Main Street in a small city. It is the connecting link between all the cellblocks, dormitories, control center, and most of the various offices. It has the width of a small city street. This area is constantly being cleaned and has a spit and polish appearance.

There was a special crew assigned to clean this corridor and, for one reason or another, they were always black. Because the corridor was so extremely wide, they had mops with handles triple the length of the normal mop handle. As a man would swing his mop, rather than keeping his hands fixed in a stationary position, as a person normally does, extending the arm and then pulling the mop back, he would let the handle slide through his hands so that the mop would keep moving and he would hold the handle slightly until it reached the very end. He would then grasp the end tightly, which would stop the movement of the mop. To pull the mop back, he would go through the reverse procedure. This was a very difficult job for men who did not know how to manipulate the long-handled mops.

However, as in many other circumstances of prison life, a prisoner will turn a liability into an asset, making his job a challenge and have fun at it.

Some men developed their job of pushing the mop into an art. The mop would be pushed with great speed, and the handle would slide through the inmate's hands so beautifully that he could execute dance steps while the mop was moving along. The different men would compete with each other as to the speed of the mop movement and the artistry and elegance and variations of their head movements, foot movements, arm movements, and body movements. Watching a crew of these men mopping the main corridor was like watching a ballet group or a modern dance troupe.

CARL WINTERS AND JOHN WILLIAMSON

One of the most famous trials to take place in the post World War II period was The United States vs. The Communist Party. The Communists were tried under a law called the Smith Act. There were eleven top Communists in the United States who were tried together and convicted. After that trial many other trials were held around the United States involving lesser Communists. The stories about the trial of the top eleven Communists together with their pictures were front-page news for many, many months. Two of the eleven convicted Communists, Carl Winters and John Williamson, were sent to Lewisburg.

These men were both approximately fifty years old, but with great differences in appearance, personality, and activities within the Communist Party. They rarely associated with many others but the two of them were inseparable. They minded their own business, antagonized no one, did their jobs to the best of their ability, and all in all served their sentences without much incident. They were both assigned to jobs that kept them away from the general prison population, doing clerical work in remote offices. Carl Winters was clerk typist in the paint shop and John Williamson had the same job in mechanical repair. Any semi-intelligent person could have handled these jobs easily. For Carl and John, the boredom and burden of serving time was increased greatly by the lack of challenge in their jobs.

Carl was the leader of the Communist Party in the State of Michigan and that part of the country. He was about five feet nine, broad shouldered, bull necked, and had thick, close-cropped gray hair. He was a very strong looking man, with thick forearms and strong hands. Without knowing his employment in his early years, one would have guessed that he could have been a steel worker or a plumber. The most obvious and effective part of Carl Winters was his speech. Carl never spoke moderately. He threw each word out as if it were on a catapult. He spoke with a deep resonant voice. There was a cannon-like boom to everything he said. He never spoke fast and he rarely spoke loud. In a crowd of talking inmates, if Carl was saying something that he wanted heard, he was heard. In a calm discussion among two or three men on any subject, his face would show the intensity of what he was saying, and his choice of words would grip the listener. To Carl nothing was trivial or minor. To him, if it was worth speaking about, it was worth speaking about with enthusiasm, and everyone around him listened. Even if I didn't agree with what Carl was saying, which was frequently the case, I was absorbed in watching and listening to him speak. Carl and I had many discussions pertaining to communism, democracy, and the American way of life. We were poles apart in our opinions on all these subjects. He was a dedicated Communist and a leader of his party. I, as an individualist in all respects, and especially after my years of regimentation, needed the total freedom that America has always offered.

In extreme contrast to Carl, his colleague and ever-present companion in the exercise yard was John Williamson. John was everything that Carl was not. He was a short, fat, flabby-faced person in rimless glasses. Even his clothing didn't seem to fit him properly. I think the reason was that his legs were so short in proportion to the rest of his body that his pants always looked too large on him. Johnny was from Scotland and he still talked with a Scots burr. He had the appearance of a minor bookkeeper. His speech was ineffectual. He was an unemotional man. I don't believe I ever saw him sad or happy, angry, or pleased. He conducted his life in Lewisburg very methodically, as I can imagine he had conducted his work within the Communist Party. His position within the Communist Party was that of national leader of the labor movement. In any organization it takes many types to make the wheels hum. There is the flamboyant man on the podium and there are the men behind the scenes, the brains, the organizers, and the workers.

Johnny never talked much about his personal life, but Carl Winters would occasionally prod him into relating some interesting incident to me. Everyone noticed and admired Carl and Carl knew from past experience that people considered Johnny a nonentity. Carl respected and admired his friend very much and after I became friendly with the two of them he wanted me to understand and appreciate John Williamson as he did.

On a particularly dreary day, the three of us were walking in the exercise yard and a discussion came up about a recent strike that was in the newspapers. Carl said, "Johnny, tell Miskin how you used to handle strikes in the old days."

Johnny said "Nah, that was a long time ago, a long time ago."

Carl said, "Tell him. It will be interesting to Miskin. He doesn't know about these things."

John said, "Well, I will tell you one story that was the beginning of my strike organizing." He said, "Back in the old days, when we didn't have laws to protect us, organizing unions was a very dangerous and difficult job. There was a particular garment factory in the New York East Side that had resisted all our efforts to make the working conditions better. All of our people who were trying to institute reform were fired immediately and were blacklisted from other factories. We determined that we had to make a cause célèbre out of this particular case. Otherwise, we were finished. This factory was the biggest and the harshest. We didn't expect to have any real success. The best we could hope for was publicity. The first step was to notify the management that we wanted a meeting of the workers to discuss the working conditions. As we anticipated, the request was ignored. The next step was to let management know that we were notifying the New York newspapers that we were going to form a picket line in front of the building to prohibit anyone from entering to go to work. The New York papers cooperated with us, not out of sympathy with our cause, but because they thought there would be bloodshed.

"Early in the morning, the men who had been fired for trying to institute reforms formed a picket line. As the whistle blew for the workers to start work, as we anticipated, the police arrived, arrested the men, and the workers entered the building. The following day we called the newspapers again and we guaranteed that there would be bloodshed. We selected our toughest young men to block the entrances and they promised that they would not be arrested peaceably. As the newspaper cameras captured the gory scene, our outnumbered young men fought the police and were bloodied with the nightsticks of the police. The situation was building up to what we wanted.

"The following day we once again notified the newspapers to cover the scene of the strike. The papers were now completely cooperative because everything we had promised them had come about.

We indicated that what had happened the day before was a Fascist slaughter and that our people would not tolerate a repetition. We told them that the police would need an army to take our men this day.

"We hired all the bullies and riff-raff we could find. It was as effective as a Hollywood set. The rough and tough of New York City stood by the gates with blackjacks, lead pipes, and bricks in their hands. The police department also came prepared. Rather than foot patrolmen, mounted police on horseback were brought. As the captain in charge of the police announced to the men that they were under arrest and would be wise to surrender peaceably, the fight began. The police on horseback didn't relish their job, but they were fighting for survival. They realized that the hoodlums opposite them would not hesitate for one moment to bash their heads in. The police charged against the enemy, using their nightsticks and very effectively using their horses to trample the toughs. Dozens of men were seriously injured. This had been the bloodiest and most notorious battle for union reform that New York City had ever seen.

"As the preceding events had been taking

place, the top union leadership had a serious dilemma. At what point should they give in? Had they served their purpose by getting publicity in the New York papers with pictures of bloody heads and police on horseback charging? Was that enough, or should they go further?"

Carl Winters at this point interrupted the story and said, "Now, listen to what happened next. This was Johnny's idea from the very beginning."

Johnny continued. "The following day the newspapers were notified once more. Everyone wondered what might be next. What could possibly be bloodier that what had taken place the day before? What was the next move in this chess game? The union organizers promised the papers that if they would have a full staff of photographers present they would capture something that the newspaper readers of America had never seen before. The New York Police Department, knowing what had transpired the previous day, could only imagine that a veritable army would be present on this day. What could the union do that would be more destructive than the clash of the hoodlums with the police? The Mayor was contacted and emergency preparations were made at nearby hospitals. As the hour approached, mounted police with reinforcements from throughout New York City lined up for what might develop.

"Hundreds of old automobiles from every direction approached the factory site. Out of the automobiles came women of every age and size – Italian, Jewish, and Irish women, first and second generation immigrants from every country in Europe. These women had worked in this or a similar garment factory and amongst them were wives, mothers, and grandmothers of the mounted police. The women lined up in front of the gates. There were old women wearing old-country babushkas and scarves, and each woman carried a baby in her arms, either her own, a grandchild, or a baby borrowed for the occasion.

"The leader of the women, backed up by the mass of female protesters and their infants, shouted to New York's finest. She raised her fist. She spat at them, and she shouted, 'Charge us with your horses! Beat us with your nightsticks! Trample the babies, damn you!!'

"Not one uniformed policeman moved. When the commanding officer, in a sickly voice, suggested to his men that they approach gently and remove the women, not one man moved.

"The factory was closed and it remains closed. The organizers had broken the will of management and of the police."

GOODBYE LEWISBURG

The morning of my departure from Lewisburg I was filled with mixed emotions. Obviously, leaving the penitentiary was the greatest day of my life, and yet, so much had happened to me within these walls in the past five years. As I entered the quarantine area, through which inmates arrived and departed, the lieutenant in charge of the federal prison bus called out the names. We lined up in military style in a column of two's. A guard then approached us and handcuffed the inmates together in pairs. The last time I had worn handcuffs I had been brought to Lewisburg. There is no way that I can honestly recall my true emotions as we were lined up, handcuffed, waiting to board the bus, and I doubt that at that moment I could have explained them. It was a feeling of mental and emotional paralysis. As we were ready to walk out the prison door to board the bus, my name was called. I, and the man handcuffed with me, walked over towards the guard. Without saying a word, he took out his keys and unlocked the handcuffs. When you have lived for so long under rigid authority and a sudden change takes place, your first instinctive reaction is fright. Something is being changed. Something has gone wrong. Perhaps they have denied my parole. Perhaps I am not being transferred after all. Perhaps I have been framed on some violation and they are going to put me in the hole. Within a half a minute a thousand thoughts chase through your mind. I asked the guard, "Why are you doing this?"

With a slight smile, he said, "You'll find out."

The man to whom I had been handcuffed was handcuffed to someone else, and the two of them marched into the bus and left me standing behind. At this point, I was in a state of frenzy. Then I saw a guard, who was an old friend of mine, walking toward me from the office. He smiled and said, "Miskin, we're making you trustee on this bus ride."

I understood what he meant. This was a favor that he was doing for me on my last day. I recalled what the trustee had done on the bus ride to Lewisburg. A convict, whether in prison or on a prison bus, lives for small favors or opportunities that the other men do not have. Everything is magnified far beyond its importance. The main benefit of being trustee on a prison bus is that the trustee is not handcuffed to anyone. If he has to go to the toilet, he doesn't have to bring his handcuffed buddy with him. At lunchtime, he walks up and down the aisle and hands out the lunches. Since he passes out the beverages, he can have all he wants to drink. As small as these things are in the big outside world, to a prisoner they added up to a very substantial plus.

    I shook hands with my old friend and thanked him, and I walked into the bus.

DREAMS

For many years after leaving Lewisburg I had a recurring dream. In my dream the police were pursuing me and I was running down city streets, through alleys, and over fences. I would see myself hiding in basements and dark corners, and again running and running, with the police constantly in pursuit of me. In my mind I knew that I had committed no crime and had done nothing wrong, yet I was totally convinced that for whatever reason the police were pursuing me, there was absolutely no way that I could persuade them of my innocence. I was sure that they would catch me and take me back to Lewisburg.

During these same years, my co-defendant had a different recurring dream. In his dream he was still in Lewisburg. One day after looking at a calendar, he realized that he should have been given a parole hearing several years earlier. In a panic, he presented the oversight to the officials, but no one would listen. He pressed his demands with every official in Lewisburg. They all pretended that they believed him and said they would look into the matter, but nothing ever happened.

CODE NAME "DUNG"

Buried in the files of the Federal Bureau of Prisons in Washington, D.C. is a report of intrigue, the facts of which are so far-fetched that they would strain the imagination of the average moviegoer. Yet, the story is true. These facts, until now, have remained unknown.

In the early 1950s, in the federal penitentiary at Lewisburg, Pennsylvania, a continuous battle of wits took place between the Jewish inmate group and the Nazi and/or lunatic fringe types. The leader of the Nazi/lunatic fringe was Douglas Chandler, a convicted traitor who was serving a life sentence for Nazi collaboration during World War II. He had broadcast Nazi propaganda from Germany.

Chandler told everyone, "Call me Doug." The Jewish inmates always referred to him as "Dung."

A group of Jewish inmates hatched a plot against Chandler to retaliate for the harassment he constantly fermented to make life miserable for the Jews. In its inception, the plot was probably a way of helping to ease the burden of monotony we all suffered from as much as it was a means of hitting back at Chandler. Tricks were always being thought up to confuse and embarrass the Chandler group.

There were three leaders of this particular conspiracy. Mike Sandor was a C.P.A. in civilian life and a decorated war hero of the French Foreign Legion for acts of heroism in Indochina. Ernst Kluge was born in Poland, had served in the U.S. Army during World War II, and had been a civilian intelligence agent for the United States Army in Vienna after World War II. He was a master of cryptology and was fluent in several languages. He had been the interpreter when the movie *The Third Man* starring Joseph Cotton and Orson Welles was filmed in Vienna. The third leader of the trio was Mendel Moscowitz, a glib-tongued confidence man who had a photographic memory. None of the participants involved in Code Name "Dung" was a hardened criminal, and all were anxious to maintain a good record so as to make parole at the earliest possible time. The chances that were taken by the participants can only be attributed to their dedication to the project as it developed.

Mike Sandor's story had been reported in national magazines because of the fascinating human interest aspects. As a young man he had committed white-collar crimes involving financial manipulations. To flee his legal problems, he went to France and joined the French Foreign Legion. He was sent to French Indochina where the French were fighting a war. After several years, in acknowledgement of their defeat, the French forces were pulled out of Indochina. Subsequently, the United States sent armed forces into the area, and the war these forces became embroiled in became known as the Vietnam War. Mike Sandor was wounded but survived a brutal battle in which most of his battalion was killed. He returned to France as a decorated war hero and received a military discharge. Later he married and began a new life in France.

Some time after his discharge, Sandor was requested by the French government to march with other heroes in the famous Bastille Day parade. By happenstance, an American Federal Agent was watching the parade and spotted Mike. The agent, of course, immediately proceeded to have Mike arrested. Mike Sandor was extradited to the United States, found guilty of the crimes committed prior to his glorious military career, and sentenced to

Lewisburg Penitentiary. In his possession at Lewisburg, he had a copy of a personal letter sent from Vincent Auriel, then President of France, to U.S. President Dwight D. Eisenhower. The letter requested total clemency for Mike Sandor in recognition of his heroic activities in the French Foreign Legion.

The request had been denied.

Douglas Chandler and Mike Sandor first met when Mike, because of his intelligence and education, was assigned as a teacher in the educational department at Lewisburg. Chandler was also a teacher. Today, it is hard to understand the political climate that prevailed in the United States in the early fifties. The assignment of a man, convicted of treason for propaganda broadcasts from Nazi Germany, to teach young, impressionable inmates in a federal penitentiary was acceptable to the authorities at that time. The Nazis were no longer of prime concern. Germany had been beaten. We were cooperating in West Germany's economic recovery. It was the Russians who were the bogeymen. We were in the midst of the "Cold War." Senator McCarthy's witch-hunt was in full progress, and the Communists in the United States were the headliners. Many prisoners in Lewisburg at that time were serving sentences for Communist activities, for perjury, for contempt of court, and for a variety of other left wing related convictions. Very educated, very famous men were given obscure jobs to keep them out of the public eye. But, anyone with a Nazi background, or who was part of the extreme right, was adjudged acceptable and was given kid glove treatment. The desires of Douglas Chandler carried much clout with both the officials who ran the penitentiary and the general inmate population.

The preferential treatment shown Chandler was the subject of many lengthy discussions among the Jewish inmates. The general conclusion was that he must have friends in high places. As the apostle of Nazism, it was both his duty and his joy to torment the Jews in Lewisburg at every opportunity and in every possible way. Our Jewish group (generally consisting of from fifteen to twenty men out of a total prison population of twelve to fifteen hundred) had to be constantly on the alert.

The origins of the conspiracy against Chandler got lost as time went on and more and more men contributed ideas to the plot. We all agreed that if the plan worked out ideally, our harassment of Chandler could drive him close to madness.

The idea was to convince Chandler that Mike Sandor was a professional hit man sent to Lewisburg by an Israeli terrorist organization for the express purpose of murdering him. A very persuading set of documents was forged to prove that Mike had voluntarily turned himself in to the American authorities in France. These documents indicated that Jewish influence in the American Justice Department and State Department, together with Israeli pressures, had pushed through the prosecution of Mike. These same groups had contrived to send him to Lewisburg to murder Chandler. Then, supposedly, after Chandler's death, the Justice Department Jews and their co-conspirators would request a total commutation for Mike from President Eisenhower. Persuading Chandler that world Jewry always collaborated to obtain its desired ends and that Jews controlled the U.S. government would not be difficult. He had preached this same doctrine in Nazi Germany as part of his propaganda effort to stir up hatred against the Jews. With the death of Chandler, his mission accomplished, Mike would resume his life in France as a respected citizen.

There were complicated problems in convincing Chandler that his life was in danger. The execution of the plot proceeded slowly. One of the Jewish inmates who was known to have a big mouth "accidentally" let drop that there was a hit man in Lewisburg paid to murder Chandler. The person who received the information was a known colleague of Chandler's, and there was no doubt that it would be passed on to Chandler. It was not a surprise to us when Chandler ridiculed the report as being absurd. Over a period of many months, we utilized a variety of schemes, with Jews telling third parties what we wanted them to know. It was expected that the information would be passed on to Chandler or to someone in Chandler's clique, and it was assumed that sooner or later Chandler would get so much feedback from different directions that he would eventually make his move.

The next step was to prove to Chandler that such an assassination had really been planned. We determined to use the same system again, but this time implying that the proof of the attempt was in a letter in Douglas Chandler's file in the records office. The Jewish group was aware that Chandler had a crony who had access to the personnel files in the records office. It took a long time to accomplish, but somehow stationery from the office of the Chief of the French Surétè was obtained. A letter was typed on this stationery addressed to the Warden at Lewisburg, and it was mailed from France so that the envelope bore a French postmark. The letter indicated that the Chief of the Surétè had confidential information that Mike Sandor, who had been transferred from France to the jurisdiction of the American authorities, was a professional assassin. His sole purpose in turning himself in was to be sent to Lewisburg to kill Douglas Chandler. The letter said that the assassination plot was instigated by Israeli secret strike forces and had the cooperation of the world Zionist movement. This information, the letter continued, had been brought to the attention of the writer by a cellmate of Mike Sandor at the time Sandor was still in France awaiting transfer to the States.

The plan was that the letter, with the envelope attached, would be placed in Chandler's file in the records office by one of our men. Our job at this point was to spread the rumor of the existence of the letter. Chandler's friend would then look in the file, read the letter, and report back to Chandler. Timing, of course, was crucial. Suppose, after the letter was inserted in the file, that Chandler's man didn't look in the file for a week... suppose during that period someone else examined the file. After Chandler's friend read the letter, we knew that he would report to Chandler immediately. Therefore, we had to have a man available to remove the letter from Chandler's file at once.

A series of signals was developed to indicate when Chandler would initially approach his contact in the records office and then, when the contact would leave the records office.

Once the rumors were spread to Chandler, he reacted as we anticipated. He approached his contact man in the records office and instructed him to look in the file. The man did so, and immediately went back to the education department to report to Chandler that there was, in fact, such a letter from the French Sûreté in Chandler's file. We also anticipated the next move. Chandler went straight to the warden's office and demanded an appointment at once. Any other inmate in a federal penitentiary would never dare to go directly to the warden's office and demand to see him. But, as I have explained previously, Douglas Chandler wielded considerable clout. As we expected, he gained immediate access to the warden. He demanded to know why something wasn't being done about the assassin who had been sent to Lewisburg to murder him and who continued to work cheek by jowl with him in the education department every day. The warden, of course, couldn't understand what Chandler was talking about. He replied that to the best of his knowledge there was no truth whatsoever in the story Chandler had related. Chandler, in a fit of rage, directed the warden to open the file and show him the letter.

There is no way of knowing the actual exchange of words that took place within the closed office of the warden. We learned later, from our sources in the inmate group, what happened. The warden finally did open the file to pacify Chandler. Naturally, the letter was not in the file because one of our people had already removed it. Chandler's conclusion, therefore, was that the warden himself was in league with the conspirators or had been paid off with Jewish money.

The next step was for Chandler to summon his attorney and repeat to him the whole story of the Jewish assassination plot in Lewisburg. Chandler told his attorney that he had proof that a letter had been in his file in the records office and that the warden had removed it so that Chandler could not see it. The attorney immediately contacted the warden. The warden, in total exasperation, said that Chandler must have lost his mind. Every detail of Chandler's story was so utterly ridiculous as not to even warrant an investigation. The accusation of his being a party to the plot and then covering up his involvement was final proof of the man's mental collapse.

From that time on, Chandler became a shadow of the arrogant man he had once been. You could see him nervously watching any time he saw more than two Jewish inmates together. Mike Sandor, in particular, was under surveillance at all times. Chandler always knew the details of what Mike was doing and his exact whereabouts at any given time. Chandler assumed, of course, that the warden had destroyed the incriminating letter and that nothing more could be done.

The Jewish group had not yet finished with Chandler, who by now was so obviously showing the wear and tear from our conspiracy. We started planting rumors once more. This time the rumor was that someone had recently seen the letter from the French Surétè in Chandler's file in the records office. Again, Chandler contacted his man in the records office. The whole sequence of events was repeated... someone in our group inserting the letter in the file; Chandler's henchman opening the file to see that it was there and reporting back to Chandler; finally, our man removing the letter once more.

Some time later, Rabbi Pickholtz, who visited the Jewish group periodically, sent an advance notice to every Jewish inmate that there was to be a meeting. He requested everyone to come. I shall never forget that meeting. As the rabbi called it to order, he was angry, and yet, at the same time, a little smile played around his Jewish mouth. His words to us were that he had been summoned to see the warden about some wild and ridiculous story. The warden told him that he had no idea what in the world was going on. However, if it weren't stopped immediately, there would be very unpleasant ramifications for all concerned. Obviously, there was no proof of any wrongdoing by any member of the Jewish community. However, the warden was starting to get pressure from headquarters in Washington, D.C. The warden suggested to the rabbi that he meet with us and put an end to the cat and mouse game we were playing with Chandler.

Rabbi Pickholtz's final words to us were, "I don't want to know what is going on, but whatever it is, please put a stop to it because it is getting out of hand."

THE LIVING QUARTERS IN LEWISBURG

There were various types of housing units in Lewisburg. A new man coming from quarantine would either be assigned to a dormitory, which contained approximately forty men and had its own toilet facilities and showers, or he would be assigned to a cellblock. Each cell in the cellblock contained its own toilet and washbowl. The officials encouraged most inmates to start out in a dormitory. With good conduct, in time they could move upward into semi-honor dormitories, and then eventually into honor quarters. An inmate who started out in a cell would remain there for his entire sentence. Generally the type of inmate assigned to a cell was a troublemaker or a person the officials felt needed protection from the other inmates. Known homosexuals and, occasionally, an inmate who insisted that he could not live in a dormitory with all the other prisoners, were also assigned to cells.

Dormitory living is a very difficult experience unless you happen to be the type of person, of which there were many, who likes to gather in groups, boast of criminal activities, brag about sexual conquests, and talk loud and ugly. An inmate who found the presence, appearance, language, and noise of the others unpleasant, had no place to escape. There was no place to read in privacy, to think in privacy, or to sleep in peace. Physical attacks and the tormenting of weaker men took place every night. It is a very difficult adjustment period for a newcomer to prison life. If you survive the period of dormitory living without physical or emotional damage, retain full control of your self, and your record remains unblemished, you have pretty well succeeded in establishing yourself in your new life.

After several months, with good conduct, an inmate is eligible to move up to what is known as semi-honor quarters. It is impossible to describe the unbelievable elation and appreciation that can come from such a modest change. The semi-honor dormitories are absolutely identical to the other dormitories, with only one exception. This exception is that around each bunk is a thin metal partition that surrounds the bunk on three sides and stands approximately four feet high. It is known as a cubicle. In contrast to the open dormitory where people are constantly sitting on your bunk and walking between the bunks, no one enters an inmate's cubicle. It is his turf and his home. He can still hear all the same noises and is subject to the same harassment and ugliness, but he doesn't have to look at it. He can lie on his bunk and the sight of the ugly world around him is closed off. Unless a person has personally experienced this minor change, it is impossible to imagine the difference it can make to an inmate in terms of privacy.

The next step up in prison life is the honor quarters. The honor quarters are of two varieties – a large cell consisting of from four to eight men or an individual cell for one inmate. Both types of cells have solid oak doors, which are not locked, and there is a small glass pane in the door. In each case toilet and shower facilities are down the hall. The large honor cells are in one cellblock and the individual cells in another. The honor quarters are the most luxurious form of living in Lewisburg. There is total privacy in an individual cell and no one enters the cell without an invitation, not even an officer. An officer will knock before coming in. He does this, not out of courtesy, but because it is an unwritten rule that if an inmate comes into your cell without your invitation, you have the right to assume he is coming in to attack you, and you do whatever you have to do to protect yourself. An officer entering your cell doesn't want to be mistaken for an attacking inmate, so he knocks first, gets your attention, and shows his uniform. The door is always unlocked unless there is an emergency of some sort in the institution, and then everyone is locked in. The cell consists of the bunk, a small metal cabinet to contain your personal effects, which opens to form a tray-stand so that you can write letters on it, and a washbowl with a mirror. In both the large honor cell and the individual honor cell there is one window so that you can look outside. This might seem like a very austere and bare home to a non-prisoner, but to someone who has come up the ladder of dormitory, semi-honor dormitory, and finally to the open cell in honor quarters, it is luxurious living.

The inmate who initially chose, or who was forced to stay in a cellblock rather than start in a dormitory, has his toilet in his cell. He is allowed to shower only twice a week regardless of how dirty his type of work may be. The showers are located in the main clothing issue area where he receives his clean clothes and towels. It is not a very pleasant existence. However, as I have indicated earlier, there are men who choose this voluntarily rather than expose themselves to all the ugliness that they must contend with in dormitory life.

SNAGS

The first time I met Snags Lewis was in the District of Columbia jail. He had just been sentenced for gambling activities. He was reputed to be the kingpin of all illicit gambling in the Washington, D.C. area and his trial had been well publicized. Our contact was rather limited and he was transferred to Lewisburg about a month before I was.

He was the physical image of what television and movie viewers have been led to expect the head of a gambling empire to look like. He was a short, fat man with a very fat face and short, stubby arms. The American media has projected the leader of a gambling syndicate as always being involved with racketeering and other illicit activities, including drug traffic and prostitution. This was not the case with Snags, to the best of my knowledge. Snags' involvement was solely with gambling activities. He was a very uneducated man and he spoke the language of the gutter. He had crawled out of one of Washington's worse neighborhoods the hard way. In meeting him for the first time, you would assume that he was a stupid lout. However, Snags had one of the quickest minds of any man I have ever known. He had an animal instinct in observing people and analyzing them. He could size up a person in two minutes and know their strong points and their weak points. This was his stock in trade. In the gambling world there is no such thing as a Dun and Bradstreet rating. You don't check a man's credit on a computer, and you don't ask for bank references. There is a grapevine of intelligence amongst the gambling fraternity and it is known whether a man pays his gambling debts, but basically it is a one on one relationship. Either you accept a large bet or you don't accept a large bet, based on a handshake or frequently a telephone call. Snags was a master of knowing just how far to go with any man, who to trust, and who could not be trusted. In contrast to the picture of a gambling czar portrayed on the media, he was one of the kindest and gentlest men I have ever known in my life. He would never harm anyone physically, and had great fear of physical harm to himself. He was a soft touch for anyone who had a sad story. Snags understood his limitations very well, and his strengths. He was always eager to have the opportunity to do a favor for someone financially, or otherwise, because he understood human nature and the give and take of life. By doing favors for others, he would be in a position to call back these favors at a future time. He needed to be liked and many loved him. He needed admiration, and he received admiration from people inside and outside his profession because of the favors that he could do and would do.

On my first day in Lewisburg, I was walking into the mess hall when an inmate rushed over to me and handed me two packs of cigarettes. I was startled because in prison I had already learned that no one does you favors without a specific reason. I couldn't imagine why anyone would be handing me cigarettes. Upon arrival in Lewisburg, all personal effects are confiscated. Generally it takes a couple of weeks before the bookkeeping is straightened out and any monies that you may have are placed in your commissary account and you are able to purchase cigarettes and other items. Therefore, during the very difficult time of transition, you don't even have the benefit of a cigarette to smoke.

I asked the man why he was giving me cigarettes and he said, "Snags sent them."

On my first Sunday in quarantine we were notified that all Jewish inmates would be allowed to go to Jewish services. I went and Snags was there. For some unknown reason, Snags had taken a liking to me and had decided to take me under his wing. In a penitentiary the one true celebrity amongst the inmate population is a racket leader or someone high in the gambling world. Snags had received a tremendous amount of publicity during his trial and many inmates at Lewisburg received the Washington, D.C. newspapers. On his first day in Lewisburg he was approached by dozens of men who were very eager to make his acquaintance and offer him physical protection. They wanted to assist him in any way they could solely for the purpose of getting to know him and winning favor in his eyes so that after their release they could look him up and benefit from his friendship.

Upon being released from quarantine, I was assigned to a dormitory rather than a cellblock. The associate warden had strongly recommended that with the long sentence facing me I should start out in a dormitory. By proving my ability to live with other men without conflict I could work my way up the ladder eventually into honor quarters. It so happened that Snags was in the same dormitory. The atmosphere of the dormitory is horrible. At least in a cell, when you came back from your day's work you had privacy. In prison, privacy was the part of your existence most looked forward to. At work unpleasant, belligerent people always surround you. During the eating periods the same type surrounds you. Only when you are in a cell alone at night can you close off the prison world. In a dormitory the horrors of prison life really begin when you come back from work. Forty to sixty men are confined together in a close area. Every one of these men has a trigger temper, anxieties, emotional problems, and is filled with frustration. You share common toilet facilities; the strong pick on the weak; the mean agitate the nervous; and the bullies attempt to subjugate everyone around them, in every possible way. It is here that small groups gather and form cliques. Fortunately for me, Snags was treated as a royal personage. He was catered to by the toughs, and because he was a gentle soul and a nice person, well liked by the nicer element.

The high point of status was to be invited to a party at night. The most important ingredient for a successful party in Lewisburg was an accumulation of Milky Way candy bars. The Milky Ways were broken up into small pieces and put into a large container and the container filled with hot water from the sink. I am quite sure that anyone reading about this mixture could never imagine the delight this hot chocolate gave us. The hot chocolate would be accompanied by all the cookies and crackers we could manage to get together. The food in any prison is never very appetizing. Frequently, when you leave the mess hall you are hungry as hell, and even if you aren't hungry, what you have eaten has not been very satisfying. These little parties at night before going to sleep were a big event. In a dormitory of forty to sixty men there might be four or five parties going on simultaneously. These parties are by invitation only and no one ever crashes them. The men who were not invited to the parties attempted to pretend that they could not see what was going on.

Snags, of course, was the center of these parties, for one very simple reason. He had sufficient money and sufficient guile to find out which inmates had no money in their prison accounts. He would make deals whereby he would have his contacts on the outside send these men money, with the understanding that half of their purchases would go to him, and they could keep the other half for themselves. He had many ready takers for his proposition. There are a large percentage of men in prison who have no one who cares on the outside, or if they do care, they are too poor to send money. In the fifties the maximum amount of money allowed for spending at the commissary in all the federal prisons was twelve dollars a month. For a heavy smoker, this would just about take care of cigarettes, toothpaste, and shaving materials. There was never anything left over for candies and cookies. Of course, with Snags' many fifty-fifty business partners, he had an abundance of cookies, candies, cigarettes, and cigars for his personal needs and to give out to those in his favor. This is a very effective way to win friends and influence people inside the prison walls. Obviously, as a friend of Snags' I was immediately invited to join him at these parties.

My first day in the mess hall, after I had entered population, could have been my most disastrous day in prison. Fortunately for me, Snags was next to me and straightened out a very sensitive matter. Sitting across the table from me was a very large hillbilly, who was as big as an oak tree, uneducated, and just plain mean. In Lewisburg, milk was served only once a day, at breakfast. It had originally started out as milk, but after considerable watering down, it had only the appearance of milk when it reached the inmate. Nevertheless, it was considered a delicacy. You could either drink it from the bowl or pour it over your hot cereal. After the inmates sat down at the table with their trays of food, an inmate waiter would approach the end of the table with a large container of milk and a stack of bowls. He would fill up the ten bowls with milk, and the inmates at the end would pass them down until they reached the other end of the table. Since this was my first day, I didn't know the procedure and I wound up with two bowls of milk on my tray.

At that point, the large hillbilly sitting across from me reached over and grabbed me and said, "You son of a bitch, I'm going to tear you to pieces."

It was so totally unexpected, I don't know what my reaction was. He thought that I had stolen his milk because I had two bowls and he had none. If Snags had not intervened very diplomatically, the two of us no doubt would have had a fight right on that spot. I would have been taken to the hole and the administration would have marked me as a troublemaker. My stay in prison would have been much different than it turned out to be.

Since Snags knew my adversary, all he did was say, "Hey, this is a buddy of mine, what's the matter?" He took one bowl of milk from my tray and gave it to the hillbilly.

The hillbilly, with a grunt and a smile, said, "Aw, Snags, I didn't know he was your buddy."

And that was the end of something that could have turned out much differently.

Snags and I became very, very close. He was a man who had never read anything in his life. He was too nervous to take naps and he did his time with more difficulty than any man I ever knew. He didn't pull one day at a time as everyone else did, he pulled each hour at a time and each hour was an agonizing hour. What he missed most was food. He was a fat man and he was fat because he ate a lot and what he ate a lot of was the things he couldn't get in prison – pastries, good coffee, and seafood. He missed these dearly. My sentence was four to fourteen years and his was six to eighteen months, and yet he would constantly cry on my shoulder and complain that there was just no way possible he could finish his sentence. Each day was too much of a burden for him. I found that instead of worrying about my own sentence I was constantly assisting him in doing each hour, in finding various ways to kill time, to help him along in the hours between the end of work and bedtime.

My close association with Snags had an interesting effect on me. He pulled such very hard time and he complained constantly. I was always worried about him, helping him, convincing him, and I didn't have time to worry about my own personal problems. Years later after I became one of the leaders of the institution and very sophisticated in the proper way of doing time and handling my relationships with both the inmates and the officers, I looked back to my beginning days in Lewisburg with great warmth towards this man. I realized that had he not assisted me in many difficult situations, my time in Lewisburg would have been much different.

The greatest outlet for Snags was walking. For a short, fat man, he could walk more than any man I ever met. He served fourteen months and fourteen days. The rest of the time was time off for good behavior. During those fourteen months and fourteen days at every possible opportunity he walked the track in the recreation yard without stopping, and on Saturdays and Sundays he would be there all day. This was his method of pulling time. With this unaccustomed exercise, he lost half of his fat and got in better condition than he had ever been.

His first job in Lewisburg was mopping the floor in the mess hall after meals. Using the mop in a federal penitentiary is a very difficult procedure because the mops have extremely long handles. Snags had never done any physical work. The mopper in the mess hall had to finish everything that had to be done before he could go back to his dormitory. Snags, not a strong man, not knowing how to handle any type of tools, would wind up working twice as long as anyone else to get the job done. When I moved into the dormitory with him his hands were raw from blisters from the long-handled mop. He finally determined that he couldn't take it any longer and on the advice of some of the inmates, went to the hospital and requested that the doctor not only treat his hands, but recommend to the warden that he be given a job transfer because of physical disability.

The next job that was given him was less physical, but probably the worst type of job they could have assigned to him at Lewisburg. He was on the work gang that unloaded the foodstuffs that came in to the kitchen. He lifted and carried large, heavy boxes of cans or baskets of fruits and vegetables, and each container he carried came close to giving him a rupture. The physical work was not so bad when compared to what he did when he was not unloading the trucks. He sat on a bench and waited for the next truck. Out of the eight hour workday his actual working time might only be three hours. The other five hours were spent sitting on the bench and waiting for the next truck. I would venture to say that Snags at that period of his life smoked at least a carton of cigarettes a day.

Snags used to say, "It's easy to do time in prison. All you need is a big ass and a big heart – a big ass for all the sitting around, and a big heart to take all the shit they hand you."

We talked on at least a hundred occasions about the type of job to which he should request transfer. A transfer was essential because he was quite sure he would lose his mind on his present job. Finally, we came up with an idea that we discussed and discussed again and again and again before he requested it. This job was on the outside labor gang. Since he was in prison for a nonviolent crime and since his sentence was a short one, the authorities weren't concerned about escape. There was no problem for him to get permission for a trustee's pass to work outside the walls. The outside labor gang consisted of about ten men who worked with picks and shovels. This is the type of job that Snags would never have volunteered for before Lewisburg. After questioning other inmates who were on the labor gang about how cold it got outside, how hard the physical work was, and whether they liked it, he finally determined that with his limited abilities and education, this was the best he could hope for. Certainly in comparison to the present job of unloading the vegetables and sitting on the bench all day, it had to be an improvement. It turned out to be the best move he could have made because it took him outside the walls. There was never a large amount of work that required great physical effort, and yet there was enough activity to keep him occupied. The one factor that concerned him very much was the cold. He had never in his life done outside work in the winter (or any other time) and he had a great fear of being cold. All his friends donated extra clothing and he would go to work in the morning wearing perhaps six pairs of pants, six shirts, as many pairs of underwear as he could fit on, plus many pairs of socks. He would waddle out to work in the morning looking like a teddy bear. Luckily for Snags, his foreman was a nice guard who understood Snags' physical limitations and didn't require too much of him. I feel quite sure that without this change of jobs Snags would have cracked.

As I have indicated previously, Snags was on good terms with all the power blocs. On one occasion after dinner I was walking around the dormitory alone. One of the Italians in power approached me and without saying a word reached a hand into my pocket to take out a cigarette. I grabbed his hand and asked him what the hell he was doing.

He answered, "You mean you won't let me have a cigarette?"

I said, "Not when you reach into my pocket,

no. If you ask for one, I will give you one any time, but never reach into my pocket."

I knew the rules of conduct in prison. Once these hoodlum types got the edge on you, you were finished. The first time they would reach in and take one cigarette. The next time they would take the whole pack. And from then on you wouldn't be able to call your life your own. These characters had to be set straight immediately. As soon as this incident happened, a hush went over the dormitory. Obviously, he had made a mistake and had misread me, and I had called him down in front of all his associates. In prison the only thing that many men have is the prestige they hold in the eyes of their fellow inmates. If they lose that, they have nothing. I had put him into a corner and he had to do something. Everyone around who had seen and heard the incident was aware of the problem. Snags, as I have indicated, was a very observant and astute man and a student of human nature. Immediately, he went over, got Guissepe by the hand, took him over to the group that was sitting and eating his Milky Way cocoa mix, and pretended that nothing had happened.

That evening before lights out, Snags came

up to my bed and he said, "Miskin, what am I going to do with you? You are going to get yourself killed and you will probably get me killed besides. You can't do things like that in here." He said, "Do you know the mumbling and grumbling that's going on with those guys? I am doing my best to keep things quiet, but for God's sake, keep away from him because this could explode at any time."

Fortunately, nothing else ever happened.

Snags and I regularly went to Jewish services together. His religious background was as sparse as mine, but it made no difference. We read the indicated portions of the service and we had a time of camaraderie with our fellow Jews. We could relax, tell Jewish jokes, reminisce about the better days, and generally unwind because there were no hardened criminals amongst us who wanted to do us harm.

The procedure of electing the Jewish leadership in Lewisburg was simple. We had no chaplain, only a visiting rabbi who came to see us periodically. There was an official election of a president and a vice-president of our group under the direction of the rabbi, who counted the ballots. The warden was notified of the election results. The president and vice-president would remain in office, not for a fixed term, but until they went home or were transferred. At that time another election would be held. There was one occasion when both of our leaders had made parole. There was one man, Lenny Katzman, who was a natural to become president because of his qualifications. His assistant, or vice-president, did not really have any authority or responsibility, but it was necessary to have this position filled in the event of the president's departure before another election could be held. To my shock, Snags nominated me for vice-president.

I told him, "Snags, I don't want that job. I am not qualified for it. I don't know anything about it. I haven't had that much religious training. I wouldn't know what to do."

His answer was, "Do what I tell you, Miskin. You have got a long sentence. You'll learn what to do. And it will look good on your record."

Since there were no real favorites for this position, and there were several men nominated, by fluke I got the job. Little did I know at that time that in a matter of months Katzman would be transferred to another institution, and I would be the leader. At that same time, our visiting rabbi moved to another city and it was a long time before he was replaced. There was no means for us to hold another election.

Snags, this little fat guy who was considered by the press, the general public, and probably a majority of the inmates in Lewisburg to be a ruthless rackets man, was in reality a very tender, soft, kind, and considerate person. There is one thing you learn very well in prison – that what a man is reputed to be is not necessarily so. It is in prison that a man's true nature often comes out... the most evil and cruel, or the most gentle and kind. The inmate is stripped of all exterior camouflage and the real "you" shows. Frequently, the worst comes out, but occasionally a man finds that this is his finest hour.

TOO MUCH OF A GOOD THING

One night when I was sleeping in my dormitory, I felt a hand touch mine and I jumped up out of bed. It was my little friend, Mike. Mike Pappas was in prison for illegal entry into this country. He was a Greek national and had jumped ship in New York. The little English he knew was learned in prison. He was one of the kindest and nicest men I have ever known. Aboard ship he had worked in the maintenance department. The officials at Lewisburg utilized his knowledge for the repair of any machinery that had to be fixed, and even without knowing English, he was a wizard.

I said, "Mike, what's wrong?"

He handed me something wrapped in a brown paper bag. He said, "Here, something for you. I've got to go back to the kitchen to work now."

He left me holding the bag containing something warm inside. I went into the toilet area where there was a little light and I extracted an odd-smelling and odd-feeling object from the bag. It was a whole beef tongue. I had never seen a whole beef tongue although I had eaten sliced tongue sandwiches in delicatessens many times. I pulled off a piece of it and tasted it, and it was good. I decided to share my booty with my dear friend Snags, who was always hungry and whom I knew would appreciate the tongue. I crept up to his bed and touched him on his arm, and he jumped up.

He said, "What's wrong?"

I said, "I've got something for you, Snags."

He said, "What the hell is it?"

I said, "Let's go into the toilet."

When we got there, I took out my odd-looking piece of meat and showed it to him. He held it in his hands and examined it and said, "What the hell is it?"

I said, "It's a tongue, Snags."

He said, "Jesus Christ, the outside's like leather."

I said, "Well, I guess we have to pull this outside layer off."

As hard as we tried, it didn't peel. The only thing we could do was pull out hunks of meat with our fingers and eat it like wild animals. After Snags had filled his belly a little, he came to his senses. He said, "Where in the world did you get this damn thing?"

I said, "Mike brought it to me."

He said, "Both of us must be crazy. We are sitting in the toilet pulling out hunks of meat from this damn thing." He said, "If a guard came through the door he would put us in the hole before you could say Jack Robinson. Let me get the hell away from here and go back to sleep."

I said, "Take some with you, Snags."

He said, "I don't want to look at that damn thing anymore. Get rid of it." He looked at me and said, "What are you going to do with it?"

I said, "I'm going to flush it down the toilet."

He said, "That's a good idea." And piece by piece I tore the tongue apart so that it would be small enough to flush in the toilet. We both slept very well that night.

THERE ARE GUARDS, AND THERE ARE GUARDS

A penitentiary consists primarily of three things: the physical buildings, the inmates, and the guards. The physical buildings may be old or modern, maximum security or minimum security, but the inmates and guards are always a mixture of human beings, a combination ranging from the best to the worst. In Lewisburg the guards were no different than in any other penal institution. The primary and ever-present function of the custodial staff, as they are officially known, is security, or in plainer terms making damn sure that no one escaped.

The method of determining if everyone is present in a prison is a procedure called "count." There are routine counts that are held throughout the twenty-four hour daily period at regular intervals. There is a count held first thing in the morning. When the whistle blows, all men in dormitories must be standing in front of their bunks. In a cell with a solid door, the inmate must be standing with his face in front of the small glass pane in the door. All men are counted as they enter mess halls and when they leave mess halls. The guards supervising the hospital know at all times how many men are within the area. Since frequently it is necessary for an inmate to travel from one part of the institution to another, he is issued a pass indicating the time he left. When he arrives at his destination, the guard in charge enters the arrival time on the pass. It is known by the officials approximately how long it should take to go from one part of the prison to another. If a longer period of time is involved than should be, a very good explanation is required.

During both day and night surprise counts are frequently held. You hear officers in all directions shout, "COUNT!" and at that point the inmate freezes where he stands. No one is allowed to move during the count procedure. Many, many times, because of incorrect counting, or perhaps a man sleeping in some obscure corner, or just plain human error, the count does not come out correctly. Immediately, another count is called for. It is always possible in a penitentiary, and it is always assumed by the officials, that someone is or will be trying to escape. After the count comes out incorrectly several times, the officials become extremely agitated, belligerent, and edgy. First, there is the understandable fear on the part of each officer that he might have made an incorrect count and will look like an incompetent to the higher officials. Also, there is always the possibility that at this particular count there is, in fact, an escape in progress. This is a time that all inmates understand that humor is out of order. No jokes. No horseplay. This is a deadly serious business. Finally, when the count comes out correctly, everyone is relieved. If the count, after repeated recounts, does not come out, everyone in the institution is ordered to his cell. Then, immediately, it is determined who the missing inmate is.

Inmates in any institution are like amateur psychologists. They observe the guards constantly. The guards, supposedly, are analyzing the inmates, but generally speaking the inmates have analyzed the guards much more thoroughly. They know the weaknesses and strengths of each one.

A guard who was in charge of clothing issue from time to time had a pilot's license. Many of us learned that his greatest interest in life was flying a small plane at the nearby airport on weekends and talking about airplanes whenever he had the opportunity. The life of a prison inmate is so uneventful and so boring that any change becomes very important, particularly a change in his personal clothing. There is not much variety – just the prison shirt and pants, belt, underwear, socks, and shoes. As a rule of thumb, no matter how tattered and worn or ill fitting these items of clothing may get, it is very difficult to secure replacements. On many occasions I have been to the clothing issue area and requested a new pair of pants or shoes and have been denied because the officer felt that there was still a lot of wear in them. I learned that the officer who was a pilot was an easy mark if he was handled correctly. The trick was, immediately upon entering his domain, to start talking about airplanes and flying. If you were smart, you would do a little prior research on the subject so that you could discuss it intelligently. As this guard talked, his imagination would soar, and instead of being in the dreary prison atmosphere, he would be in the wild blue yonder doing what he liked best. After a few respectful questions as to how he would handle certain situations, giving him an opportunity to demonstrate his knowledge, I would ask for a new pair of pants or a new pair of shoes. Without any further discussion, I would be issued whatever I had asked for. The men who were unsuccessful in getting what they wanted thought this guard was the meanest man in the world, but those of us who knew his secret thought he was the greatest.

Since the guard's time in prison is almost as boring as that of an inmate's, many of them tried different methods to make their working hours more interesting. There was one guard who took great pride in remembering every inmate's number. In Lewisburg all our numbers had five digits and we had approximately fifteen hundred men at any time. That is a tremendous amount of numbers to remember. It became common knowledge among the inmate population that remembering numbers was this guard's claim to fame. To stimulate the day a little more for us and also for him, anyone who passed near this guard would ask, "What's my number, Mr. Evans?" To the amazement of all around, most of the time he knew it.

There were some guards whom we rarely saw because they worked the night shift in the various towers on the wall. Occasionally, these men would come into the prison during daylight hours and we would see guards who had worked there twenty to thirty years, but whom we had never before seen.

They spent their whole working life sitting in a little guard tower on the wall at night. It was obvious that when they were assigned to the usual guard duties in the daytime they had no idea what the procedures were.

There were, of course, guards of the lowest sort, to whom tormenting the men was not sufficient. They had their own methods of taking some advantage of these poor creatures. There were not many, but there were some guards assigned to the visiting room, whose special interest were the women who came to visit their brothers, fathers, or husbands. I know of many situations where the women were secretly propositioned with the promise that the guard would make the time of the inmate they were visiting easier. Frequently, the women would receive a veiled threat that if they did not cooperate, the time of the inmate would be made very difficult. What made a situation of this type so disgusting and painful was that the women were afraid to relate these episodes to the men they were visiting. They were afraid that it would upset them to a dangerous point or cause them to get into difficulty in one way or another. Usually, when a guard was reported for such misconduct, it was because the woman contacted her attorney and her attorney then went through official channels. It was a rare occasion for inmates to have access to this kind of information. Every now and then, though, when one guard would really want to put another guard on the spot, he would let it be known to an inmate that a particular guard had been called to the warden's office and reprimanded for such conduct. The names of the inmates' wives were never mentioned because this would be a sure motive for murder.

AND THEN THERE WAS ZACHARIAH THOR

The best known and most infamous guard in Lewisburg was a lieutenant by the name of Zachariah Thor. He was referred to very descriptively and derogatorily by all the inmates as "Fats." This man could have been a character in an old James Cagney prison movie. He was a large man, well over six feet, with a fat face and a mouth that never smiled. He wore a perpetual sneer. He had a large head, thick arms, and big hands. He wore his belt low and it came below his potbelly. He loved his work and he was hated and feared by the inmates.

Zachariah Thor was not a very bright man, but he considered himself to be a superior judge of human nature and the most efficient officer in the federal prison system. He assumed that every inmate was constantly attempting to cause him personal problems by plotting an escape, involvement in sexual activities, or smuggling contraband in one form or another. He took great pride in periodically announcing to groups of inmates that whenever there were three inmates talking together, one belonged to Lt. Zachariah Thor. What he meant was that a large number of inmates were his informers. He would solicit informers by two methods. He offered to assist them in the prison in some way in return for information. If they refused to cooperate, he would promise them that he would do them harm. The other method was simply to meet them privately on occasion and pay them off with cigarettes or candy. No one ever really knew how successful his grapevine was. We all assumed that the reason he talked about it so much was to scare the hell out of us and to make us believe that it was true, when in reality his network probably was not greatly effective. He loved with a passion to see the fear in men's eyes. The fear came not only from the thought of the physical beatings that might take place, which happened only on rare occasions, but the fear of the harm that Zachariah Thor could do to them.

There was another factor that created fear. A prisoner has very little to look forward to in his prison life. The things that he values, basically, are getting the type of job that he likes, securing the type of living quarters he wants, and retaining his privileges, such as the recreation area and movies. A lieutenant in the guard force has great control and authority over all these matters and if an inmate arouses his displeasure, he finds himself in a helpless situation indeed.

It was rumored that Fats Thor had been passed over for promotion on many occasions and that men he had started with in the federal system were now captains and associate wardens. This fact surely must have added to his bitterness. His greatest pleasure seemed to be harassing and frightening inmates. He took a particular interest in me, and he must have thought about me a lot. I had become a respected and influential individual with both the inmates and the officials through my several positions as president of the Jewish group, chairman of the debating group, and secretary in the electrical shop. Thor had watched me carefully from my first day in Lewisburg. He saw my progress and he determined that he would get me. I wasn't there very long before he started his constant harassment of me. As I was walking down the wide hall one day, he pointed his finger at me and said, "Come here." He asked me for my pass to determine if I had proper authorization to be where I was and he checked the time I had left my place of origin. Then he told me to assume the position.

The position is a posture of leaning forward with your hands against the wall and your feet spread so that you are off balance and it has become familiar to most TV viewers of police stories. The inmate (or suspect) is in a rather uncomfortable and helpless stance.

Lt. Thor always carefully gave me an examination over my entire body, as well as my pockets, until he determined that I wasn't carrying anything that I shouldn't. He didn't offer me an explanation and from that time on he would at least once a week go through that procedure. He would see me in the mess hall, in the recreation area, or at work and he would stop me. Words were no longer necessary. He would point at me and point to the wall and I would assume the position.

After about two years of this procedure, he finally looked me in the eyes and said, "Miskin, I have been watching you a long time. I know you are into many things in this joint and I'm going to find out what you are involved in. Remember this – Lt. Zachariah Thor is telling you – I am going to get you."

And so this cat and mouse game continued

for many years and I didn't enjoy being the mouse one bit. As time went on and I was known as a well adjusted, stable inmate and my reputation with the higher officials increased, his frustration also increased. To my great good luck he was never able to find me in any act where he could harm me.

When I finally made parole from Lewisburg and was being transferred to another institution for release, I found out through my own sources in advance of the actual transfer, when and where I was going. One of the biggest secrets in a prison involves the transfer of men because when men are traveling on a bus, that is probably the easiest time for an inmate to escape with outside help. Therefore, in prison the officials guard transfer information more closely than any other. Due to my connections, I did find out about my transfer.

Incredibly, the day before I was to leave, Zachariah "Fats" Thor approached me, called me into a corner, and said, "Miskin, I've got something very important to tell you." He spoke in a whisper. "I'm doing you a big favor – tomorrow morning they are shipping you out." Obviously, he didn't know that I already knew about the transfer. After so many years of frustrating harassment, instead of letting me leave quietly, he decided to show me what a good fellow he was and that there were no hard feelings. I pretended that what he had told me was new information to me and I thanked him profusely. Again, I had my little victory over Thor. I knew that he would find out after I left that I had already known what he told me.

An inmate for whom I had done favors in the past had come across the official transfer papers about two weeks before my pending transfer and immediately notified me. The normal procedure for the federal prison system is that when an inmate who has had a good conduct record makes parole, he will be transferred to the institution nearest his home. This enables him to have more frequent visits with his family prior to release and assist him in making plans necessary for the start of a new life. I did not want to be transferred because I knew that I could do my remaining two months in Lewisburg without too much of a problem. Going into a new institution is always a dangerous situation. You don't know the men and the men don't know you. You have to start from scratch, and I wanted no part of that. I immediately wrote a note to my caseworker requesting a meeting to discuss my pending transfer. I received no reply, which was very unusual. I submitted another request, indicating that I had sent one previously. Still no answer. I then wrote a request to the associate warden's office, indicating that I had written two requests to my case worker with no answers, and asking him to please show me the courtesy of granting me an interview. I still did not receive an answer.

Then I took a calculated risk. I knew the associate warden quite well through my various activities over the years in Lewisburg, and I went to his office without an appointment. I told his secretary that I was there on a matter of extreme importance and that I must see the associate warden immediately. I assumed that this unauthorized act would not get me in trouble because the associate warden knew me and he knew my record, and I had made parole. After a short wait I was taken into the associate warden's office.

He said, "Miskin, sit down and calm down." He said, "You know, you're creating a hell of a lot of trouble here for us."

I said, "Why, Warden?"

He said, "Don't you think I know about the

two requests you sent in to your case worker? Don't you think I saw the request you sent to me?"

I said, "Yes, sir, I would assume that you know about it. But why am I being treated this way? I don't deserve this type of treatment. You know yourself, Warden, that I have been a model inmate. I have never caused any problems. Why is everyone avoiding me like I have the plague?"

He said, "Miskin, you know that when a prisoner is transferred it is top secret, and you are writing open interview letters requesting to discuss why you are being transferred." He said, "Tell me, why don't you want to be transferred? We are doing this because it will bring you closer to your home and if we didn't think very highly of you, if you had not been a model prisoner, we would not be going to this trouble and expense. Why don't you want to be transferred?"

I explained my concern at being a new inmate in another institution and the possibility of getting into trouble there. I respectfully requested, due to my good record, that I be allowed to stay at Lewisburg until my day of parole. The warden said that it was not possible because final transfer orders had already been sent from the federal prison system in Washington, D.C. and the orders couldn't be rescinded. He then asked the other men present in the office to leave, and he shut the door.

He said, "Miskin, we've known each other a long time and we've gotten along very well. I respect you and I think you respect me. I am going to ask you a question. As you know, having been in Lewisburg for over five years, we have many men here who are very dangerous. Security is a must. You, of all people, can understand that. It is absolutely necessary to maintain the secrecy of who is being transferred and when. Now that you are leaving prison life, tell me, please, how did you find out?"

"Warden," I said, "As you have indicated, we have gotten to know each other very well. I will explain this much to you. A person, and I am not going to tell you whether it was an official or an inmate, did me a favor by giving me this information. Now what kind of a human being would I be if I gave you his name before I left Lewisburg? I wouldn't think very much of myself, and in spite of what you say, you wouldn't think much of me either. And I think that ends the discussion, Warden."

He looked at me, smiled, shook my hand, and said, "Good luck."

It was because of this unusual set of circumstances concerning my transfer that I knew beyond a doubt that after I left Lewisburg Lt. Thor would certainly learn that I had known in advance about my transfer. He would know that I had made a fool of him by my pretense that his information was news to me.

MOSKOWITZ

One day I was walking down the main corridor to visit someone who was very sick in the hospital. Moskowitz ran over to me and said, "Miskin, I've got to talk to you."

I said, "Not now, Moskowitz, I'm in a hurry."

He said, "It's important. I've got to talk to you."

I looked him straight in his eyes and said, "All right, I'll give you a minute, but no bullshit, no bullshit, Moskowitz."

He looked at me with a sad expression on his face, and said to me, "Miskin, no bullshit, no Moskowitz."

Moskowitz was an extremely complex person and a man of unbelievable mental agility and ability. The inmates and officers never knew when he was lying and when he was telling the truth. He had a photographic memory. He could read a medical journal for fifteen minutes and quote it verbatim to a visiting doctor. At one time he had actually convinced a visiting bone surgeon that he was, in fact, an M.D. He did this by going to the hospital library immediately prior to the arrival of the doctor and reading a chapter relating to the type of bone surgery that was about to be performed. Many times in my association with him I was totally convinced that everything he was saying was a lie and that he was one hundred percent neurotic. Many other times, when I had reached the end of my patience with him, he would totally surprise me and everyone else by doing exactly what he claimed he could do.

One day we were walking around the exercise yard listening to some hillbillies play their guitars and as we passed, Moskowitz made a remark to one of the guitar players, indicating that he was using the guitar improperly. I had heard so much of his lies and pretenses over the years that at this point I grabbed the guitar, pushed it into his arms and said, "Here, you show him how to play it." To everyone's amazement, he sat down on the bench and played like a professional.

Another time we were walking in the exercise yard and he constantly gave suggestions to the men who were playing handball as to how they could improve their games. In Lewisburg, handball was one of the favorite sports because there was plenty of wall space on the thirty-foot wall that surrounded the prison. There were many excellent handball players in the institution. To the best of my knowledge, Moskowitz had never played handball in Lewisburg. He was always occupied with the bull sessions in the yard where no exercise was required at all. Annoyed, one of the recipients of his advice challenged him to enter the tournament that was being held for the best handball players. You can guess the result. Moskowitz entered and won the title.

Moskowitz was a man of about six feet, who would have been taller had he stood up straight. He stooped slightly, not because of bad posture, but because of over-developed muscles in various parts of his body. One of his many claims was that he had been A.A.U. wrestling champion of New York State. He walked slightly bow-legged, like a cowboy who has seen many years in the saddle. He had nice looking curly hair, with the face of a university professor. He was in his mid-thirties. He wore rimless glasses, which he was always polishing. He claimed this was done out of habit as he was one of the world's greatest diamond experts and he needed clean lenses to examine gemstones, as he called them. His face and facial expressions would vary depending on the mood he was in or what story he was telling. He was a great actor. When he told of his exploits as a World War II commando in the rangers, you would swear that you were looking at John Wayne's twin. In discussing his diamond cutting abilities, he would appear to be a Jewish diamond merchant with a pointed nose and squinty eyes. In describing his athletic feats, his muscles would flex and you would see the all-American boy.

Both the inmates and officials liked Moskowitz, but he had most people buffaloed. There was one lieutenant, named Zachariah Thor, who was always attempting to find some inmate in violation of one of the rules. This was his greatest gratification. He was known as a hard and tough official. One day Moskowitz was leaving the hospital after working a late shift. Since the con was second nature to him, when he came to Lt. Thor's office he asked if there were any sandwiches. He said that he was very hungry and had missed dinner because of an emergency operation. The lieutenant's office usually has bags of sandwiches and fruit for hospital personnel who have missed a meal because of their hospital duties. So that the inmates would not go to bed hungry, their names were placed on a list and the kitchen supplied food packages for the men involved. Moskowitz, of course, had not missed any meals, but he was always trying. This time when he asked Lt. Thor if he had a package for him, Lt. Thor knew for sure that Moskowitz had not missed a meal. Instead of just telling him he was not entitled to a package, he gave him a lunch bag. As Moskowitz walked down the corridor towards his cellblock, as a joke Lt. Thor called up another officer on duty and told him that Moskowitz was heading that way and had stolen a lunch bag. He told the officer to take the lunch from Moskowitz and to bring Moskowitz back.

Several of my friends happened to be standing near the officer when Moskowitz arrived and described to me the almost unbelievable con that Moskowitz worked on the officer. When the officer asked for the lunch bag, Moskowitz denied that he had it. When the officer proceeded to search him, he maneuvered the bag in such a way that when the officer searched his legs, he held it in his hand, and when the officer searched his front, he moved the bag around to another place. The officer called

Lt. Thor and said, "Lieutenant, you're mistaken. I have just shaken down Moskowitz and he hasn't got any lunch on him."

Lt. Thor told the officer, "You damn fool. I know he has it because I gave it to him."

There were many men of ability and intelligence in Lewisburg and they decided to form a debating group. Weekly meetings were held in the library and we would choose various subjects of national interest and accept volunteers to form a debating team, two on each side. Our library was more than adequate for research purposes and, obviously, we had plenty of time for study. Once a month we held a debate and the rules were according to the National Collegiate Debating Society. To our good fortune, we had a prison librarian who had been on a college debating team, and he was extremely cooperative. Mr. Smith's position in the federal prison system was very drab and the debates put a little excitement into his job. Through his efforts, permission was granted by the warden to invite debating teams from universities to come to Lewisburg and debate us on their current collegiate debating topic. There were many small colleges around the Pennsylvania area and their debating teams would come frequently. They were extremely pleased to come because they knew that they would get keen competition and it was an opportunity to have a dress rehearsal before taking on another college. No doubt there was also a strong curiosity on the part of these young college men to go within the walls of a federal penitentiary and observe convicted felons close at hand.

Over a period of time we developed such a great reputation that it became a status symbol for the college teams to come to Lewisburg and debate us. Our librarian and coach informed us one day that the famed debating team from Oxford University was in the United States and was to be at Bucknell in the near future. Bucknell was just a few minutes drive from Lewisburg. Mr. Smith used every device in his power and finally worked out an arrangement to get the Oxford team to come to Lewisburg and try us out. We had about two months' notice for this debate. Although we knew the subject of the debate, it was determined that neither Oxford nor the Lewisburg group would know which side we would debate until an hour or so before debate time. As on other occasions, the judges would be the coach from the visiting debating team, our librarian, and a neutral, who was usually a faculty member from Bucknell University.

Usually, if I was not one of the debaters, I chaired the debate, and on this particular evening I was the chairman. Considering the importance of the debate, there was no problem in choosing our representatives. Two men in our group, Mendel Moskowitz and Mike Sandor, were extremely able speakers. Moskowitz was a polished public speaker who knew how to use every part of his body for dramatic impact and emphasis and how to utilize a pause, and when to speak slowly or softly or thunderously to achieve the effect he wanted. He was a born actor. He had a vocabulary and style that was part economics professor, part Baptist minister, and part poet. He had mental agility and could attack like a German police dog.

Mike Sandor was also an unusual man in many ways. He had been a C.P.A., tax consultant, and financial wizard. When he ran afoul of the law he joined the French Foreign Legion. He was decorated for heroism in French Indochina. Eventually, he was apprehended by the U.S. government and brought back to this country to stand trial, and he wound up at Lewisburg. Mike didn't talk much.

But when he spoke, he spoke directly and with authority. He had a strong voice and he knew what he was talking about. In appearance he was short, with a paunch that was all muscle. He didn't look very impressive, which probably was one of the reasons that when he opened his mouth he made sure that attention would be drawn to him through both the power of his voice and his knowledge.

The night of the debate the library was filled to total capacity. Not only the inmates, but many of the prison employees who had rarely come to hear a debate before, were there. We followed the rules of collegiate debate. The pro side spoke first for ten minutes, followed by a member of the con side, with equal time. Then it was the pro side's turn again, and the last speaker represented the con side. There was a fifteen minute interval after the last speaker, at which time the rebuttal would take place, with the sequence of speakers reversed. The rebuttal is the most difficult part of any debate and by far the most interesting. Up to that point the speakers had been using prepared speeches. The rebuttal reveals not only the speaking ability of the debaters and the research effort, but it tests the agility of the minds of the debaters. They must either refute the facts of the opposition or counterattack with additional information. During the initial speaking time of all four participants, there was no clear winner on either side because all four men were extremely well prepared and all four were most eloquent. It was truly a night to remember.

Mike Sandor was the first speaker on rebuttal. Mike, as I said, was a fabulous speaker. However, he did not have the agility of mind, nor had he done the exacting research that his opponents had done. Therefore, his rebuttal was not very effective. The next speaker was from Oxford. He not only tore into what both Moskowitz and Sandor had said in their initial speeches with reams of documentary evidence to back up his attack, but he also slashed Mike's rebuttal to ribbons.

The next man on rebuttal was Mendel Moskowitz. I remember the scene vividly. As chairman of the debate, I sat there with a total appreciation of what I had seen and heard, an appreciation that could have only been felt by a person who had been a participant in similar debates. I relished every word, every parry and thrust of those keen minds. Even as the air in the library got a little heavy with pity for the home team, Moskowitz picked himself up from his chair and lit a cigarette, which is never done in a collegiate debate. He smiled to the judges, nodded to the audience, and with the confidence of a stalking panther, he approached the podium. Moskowitz had what he had always wanted, a large group of listeners that was practically a captive audience. They were expecting to see him shattered, but knowing Moskowitz, they were not sure what would happen. The game was not over for Moskowitz. He took a leaf from Senator Joseph McCarthy's pages. He ridiculed the opposition, accused them of insufficient research, and then forgave them for their youth and inexperience. He went on to give documented evidence from the sheets of paper he held in his hands, quoting extensively from such sources as *The New York Times*, *The Washington Post*, the *Encyclopedia Britannica,* mentioning chapter, paragraphs, and page numbers. As he threw this information into the teeth of the debaters from Oxford, the bewilderment and confusion on their faces was obvious to all. When the last rebuttal took place by Oxford, the speaker was a stumbling, stammering, incoherent, confused man. He was at a loss for words, admitted that all of Moskowitz's documentation was unknown to him, and slouched back to his chair. At the end of the debate, the crowd applauded madly for Moskowitz and the judges voted the debate a tie, as a gracious gesture to Oxford.

No one in the crowded room besides me understood what had happened. I ran up to Moskowitz as he was shaking hands and being congratulated, pulled him into a corner and said, "You son of a bitch."

He looked at me with the innocent eyes of a child and said, "What do you mean?"

I told him, "Moskowitz, I know God damn well that you made up every fact that you used in your rebuttal. The whole thing was a pack of lies and strictly the imagination of Mendel Moskowitz."

He smiled an innocent, happy smile, and said, "What's the harm?"

I said, "Don't you understand, Moskowitz? You just don't do that in a collegiate debate."

He really didn't understand what I was talking about. He was an extremely happy man. He had fooled everybody and had demonstrated his brilliant mental agility, and he had conned everyone who heard him.

STRANGE NEW WORLD

When I first arrived in quarantine, I heard two inmates talking about an officer. They said, "You better watch that hack because he shoots four or five men every day."

I said to myself, "My God, what kind of a place have I come to?" I had no way of knowing that by a "shot" they meant a disciplinary report. I actually believed that there were guards who would shoot inmates with their guns for misconduct.

* * * * * * * *

A young bookmaker came to my cellblock for his first exposure to jail life when I was in the D.C. jail. Usually, in the D.C. jail two inmates were put together in each cell and one could explain the procedures to the other. For some reason Scotty was in a cell by himself. To check whether any of the bars in the cells were loose or missing, every night the guards walked along the length of the cellblock with a metal pipe and dragged the pipe against the bars. This nightly routine made a horrible clanking sound of metal dragging against metal. Since this was Scotty's first night in jail, he imagined that the noise was caused by prisoners rioting. The following day he related this story to me.

He said that as the noise got closer and closer to his cell, he remembered scenes of prisoners rioting in old Humphrey Bogart and George Raft movies. They all took their tin cups and ran them across the bars in protest. Scotty was petrified on this, his first night in jail. What should he do? Should he join in the prison riot? He didn't even know what they were rioting about. If he didn't join in, all the hardened criminals around him would probably consider him a ratfink. He couldn't make up his mind. He had only been arrested for accepting horse bets and he would probably be out on probation in a few days. The clanking got closer and closer. Finally, he heard the noise coming from the cell next to him. Now he must make his decision. He grabbed his tin cup and started running it back and forth across the bars. He looked up and his eyes locked with another pair of eyes. They belonged to a guard, who was running his pipe across the outside of the bars.

The guard asked him, "What in the hell are you doing?" Scotty had no answer, and he crawled into his bed feeling like a damn fool.

THE LETTER

In the main corridor near the control center in Lewisburg there were two mailboxes. On one mailbox there were the words "Federal Bureau of Prisons, Washington, D.C." and the other one said, "Congressmen, Senators, and Judges." We had been told that any inmate could send a letter to any official to whom he wanted to make a complaint or write in connection with his case. We were promised that these letters were not censored, were not opened before they were received at the final destination, and that we could send as many letters as we liked. In a federal prison all regular mail going out and coming in is censored and frequently outgoing mail is returned to the inmate if the officials don't like the contents of the letter. Inmates soon learn not only that they can't trust other inmates, but that they can't trust the officials either. I became convinced that the whole mailbox gimmick was a charade and a fraud.

I had heard so many stories of men having their sentences reduced for one reason or another that I determined to write a letter to my sentencing judge. I felt that I had nothing to lose, and when you are desperate, you'll try anything. I worked on the letter for weeks until I finally arrived at what I considered to be the right combination of words. I dropped the letter in the mailbox designated for federal judges. About a week later the letter was returned to me, opened, with a brief note from the Bureau of Prisons advising me that my sentencing judge no longer had jurisdiction over reduction of sentences and that I would have to write to the United States Attorney General.

   The sentencing judge never received my letter.

YOU CAN HURT A MAN WITH A SHANK WITHOUT CUTTING HIM

The tension and friction amongst the inmates is always close to the explosion point, and men are constantly plotting to do other men harm in one way or another. Often a man will determine that instead of hurting someone physically, a greater degree of harm can be done to him through a frame-up. The victim will be put in the hole and possibly, because of this disciplinary action, fail to make parole. One of the schemes was to place a shank, which is a handmade knife, in the personal belongings of an inmate just prior to a shakedown. Another way is to make sure that an informer tells an official that an inmate has a shank hidden in a particular place. Of course, once the weapon is found, it is totally impossible for the marked man to convince the officials that he didn't know anything about the weapon. This is one of the many, many things that keep an inmate alert and frightened throughout his entire time in prison. I myself have searched my own belongings hundreds of times looking to find something that was planted.

THERE'S ALWAYS A FIRST TIME
(THE ESCAPE)

I had been in Lewisburg for approximately a year and I was living in semi-honor quarters. This is a dormitory in which each man's bunk is surrounded on three sides by a metal partition separating his bunk from the other bunks. Something happened which had never before happened in the history of Lewisburg. Three men escaped from my dormitory, went over the walls, and made a clean getaway. The escape had been very carefully planned over a period of months, and it was executed with great precision. There is a large barred window in each dormitory for ventilation purposes. The escaped men had smuggled saws from their workshops and over a period of months had managed to saw two bars through. I lived in the dormitory with these men and at no time did I ever hear any noise. I had no idea what was being planned and what was actually taking place. The escape, naturally, was talked about for months and months afterwards. As information was pieced together from what the guards said, through the grapevine the true story became known.

The inmates had replaced the bars after sawing through them and glued them together so that by appearance they looked the same as the other bars. They must have sawed the bars a few minutes at a time and hid each time a guard approached with his flashlight throughout the night. The sawing of the bars was only a small part of the total escape plan. Their method of getting over the walls was ingenious. They stole small pieces of pipe from the various maintenance shops and threaded both ends of the pipe so that the pieces could be screwed together. They hid pieces of the pipe in different parts of the prison yard. After the escape, many pieces of pipe were found that had not been taken from their hiding places and used. On the night of the escape, once the inmates got out of their second floor window, they gathered their small pieces of pipe and screwed them together to make two long poles. Since the wall was thirty feet high, the total length of the poles had to be at least that high. The poles were laid parallel to each other. At various points, perhaps two or three feet apart, holes had been drilled into the pieces of pipe so that a long bolt could be slid through the holes to make the rungs for their makeshift ladder.

It was later learned that the inmates had received no outside assistance whatever. Footprints were found in the soft farmland around the prison leading to a small village nearby, where an automobile was stolen. These men were later found in New York City in a cheap hotel and were shot down and killed in a gunfight with police.

GAMES

When an inmate starts nearing the end of his sentence, either through parole or just through expiration of time served, there is a game that is played. It is called "short-timer." According to the rules that the prisoners have made up, you become a short-timer when you have one hundred days left to serve.

There is a frequent shout from one inmate to another, "Hey, short-timer, how many days you got left?"

The reply would be, "Seventy-five and a get-up" or twenty-two and a get-up" or "three and a get-up." The get-up was the day he was leaving, because he didn't have to serve that day, he just had to get up in the morning.

The most disgusting game I have ever seen played in prison is a game called "the dozens." You would have to see this to believe that men would willingly play such a game for the sole purpose of escaping from boredom. I have no idea of the derivation of the term "dozens." The rules of the game were that the two participants had to be friendly.

The object was for one man to say something to the other man to make him so angry that he would lose his composure and want to attack him. The winner would be the one who would show such self-restraint that he wouldn't indicate anger at what the other one said to him. It is not necessary to go into details of what taunts were exchanged, but they would start out with one accusing the other of minor unmanly attributes. As the game progressed, the criticisms would get harsher and uglier, with mothers, wives, sisters, and daughters slandered. The obscenities would get so foul that after awhile one man would reach the end of his endurance and grab the other man as if he were ready to tear his heart out. He would be the loser. Then everybody would laugh, and two other men would start playing the game.

VICTOR J. JEROME

Victor J. Jerome was convicted and sent to prison under the Smith Act because he was one of the leading Communists in the United States.

He was a man of about seventy when I met him, very small of body, with a soft, tender, gentle voice. He was a well-known author and playwright. Victor had surrounded himself, before Lewisburg, with people from the arts – theatre people, authors, and artists of various kinds. He worked at home in a quiet and scholarly atmosphere. Everything he needed for his work was close at hand – his typewriter, his files, his library.

When he came to Lewisburg, like every other new inmate, he was put in solitary confinement, in quarantine. The purpose of quarantine is to keep the new inmates separated from the general prison population for thirty days to undergo medical, psychological, and educational examinations. During this period, the inmate lives in a totally bare cell except for a bed, a toilet, a washbowl, and a metal cabinet. It is the loneliest portion of any inmate's prison life. For a man of younger years or one who has been accustomed to a rougher existence, this thirty-day period is hard enough to bear. For Victor, deprived of the comforts of home, his books, his friends, his cultural outlets, quarantine was almost a disaster.

He told me the story one day of how he survived the thirty-day quarantine period. One of the most insignificant of material things saved him. Victor didn't have a notebook in which to write his thoughts, but he had a pencil he had somehow gotten. He picked up scraps of paper when he went to the mess hall, and then he'd sit on his bed and write notes on the scraps of paper to try to record his feelings about the present and his hopes for the future. As some men find relief in physical exercise, Victor found relief in writing. In quarantine he was without all the things he needed for writing, so he utilized what he had – scraps of paper and a pencil. However, in order to have continuity of thought, one piece of paper must be followed by another in sequence, like the pages in a book. To keep the pages in proper order, he would stack them neatly in the corner of his cell. Invariably, when the door was opened (in quarantine the door was of solid oak), his notes were strewn all over the cell. He tried to get around this problem by carrying his notes in his pocket, but that didn't work out very well.

One day, when it was his turn to mop the cell, he discovered something in the corner under his bed that changed his whole life. His discovery was only a paper clip. Such an insignificant item, meaningless to most people, but it gave Victor a method of holding his notes together so that they could form a manuscript. In telling me this story, tears came to his eyes in remembrance of the impact and joy of his momentous discovery.

This story was Victor's method of relating to me the extent of his despondency during his period of quarantine. If a paper clip had such significance for him and gave so much uplift and purpose to his days, he must have been emotionally at rock bottom.

One day Victor and I were walking around the outside yard, just the two of us. Something happened that reflects the character of this gentle, tender man. He was discussing a very deep and involved work of literature with his usual enthusiasm, and gesticulating with his hands. By accident, his hand hit the pipe he was smoking and some hot ashes from the pipe landed on my bare chest. Victor was so upset that he had been the cause of pain to me that he cursed his pipe. This pipe was more than just a pipe. It was a personal possession that had been a part of his life for many years and the only thing he had with him at Lewisburg that was a part of his past. He cherished his pipe, yet his anger was directed at it because it had hurt me.

As we continued our stroll, the exact same thing happened again, and this time he was so outraged at the pipe that he took it from his mouth and threw it across the yard. This was not the act of a crazy man. It was his way of asking forgiveness for having harmed me.

Of course, I ran across the yard and retrieved the pipe, and we continued our walk and conversation.

WHO IS A JEW?

In Lewisburg the method of determining who was Jewish was very simple. We needed no rabbinical council to make the decision for us. If an inmate stated on the official forms that he was Jewish, he was automatically Jewish.

The Protestant chaplain, who was technically in charge of the Jewish group, notified me whenever a Jewish inmate came to Lewisburg. He would also issue me a pass to enable me to see the new arrivals, who were not allowed to have any contact with the general population. Usually, the initial discussion I had with a new inmate was very limited. I would explain what my position was, indicate that we had religious services on Saturday mornings, and that on Sunday mornings, from time to time, we were visited by a rabbi. Those Sundays when the rabbi did not come we just had a social get-together. Without exception, during the five year period of my imprisonment, every Jew who came to Lewisburg and who stated on the record that he was Jewish, attended either Saturday or Sunday services with our group. Upon occasion, there were men, who for reasons of their own, did not state they were Jews. Of course, we had no contact with them as a part of the Jewish group.

One of my most interesting contacts in all my years in Lewisburg in an initial talk with a new, quarantined inmate took place with an elderly gentleman by the name of Leopold Licht. I knew this man but a few weeks when he was transferred to the prison farm shortly after he made parole, but I shall never forget what passed between us.

I met Leopold Licht and introduced myself and invited him to join our group. He was a very wealthy man from Baltimore, Maryland who was serving a year and a day for a white-collar crime. He explained to me that although he had registered as a Jew, he had had no Jewish associations for maybe forty years.

He said, "I married a gentile woman and my children were raised in the Christian faith. I am a Jew by birth only, with no affiliation or involvement in the Jewish social life or religious world."

He said he appreciated my invitation very much but felt that under the circumstances he would be out of place. I said, "Leopold, I understand what you are telling me. But you registered as a Jew. You didn't have to. You could have stated 'no religion.' If you registered as a Jew, you must feel somehow that you are a Jew. Let me explain something to you about prison life. This is a very harsh atmosphere. You are a gentle person, a businessman. You are getting up in years. You have never been exposed to the way of life that you will find here. Come to our services. You'll meet other Jews in similar circumstances to yours. We are not primarily a religious group. We are a group of men who come together, say a few prayers, and for a couple of hours find an escape from the ugly reality of the life we lead here. There is a pleasant conversational give and take between fellow Jews. No one there will care anything about your past. You will immediately have fifteen or twenty friends who you will feel comfortable with, who will care about your welfare, who will help you if they can. You'll need that kind of relationship. Please don't deprive yourself of this opportunity."

He said, "I appreciate so much what you are saying, but you don't understand. I wouldn't even know what words to say in a prayer book. I haven't been to a temple since I was a child."

I said, "Leopold, we will show you. Please come."

He came to our services and when he walked in I introduced him to the other inmates who were there. I said, "This is Leopold Licht. Leopold, I would like you to meet..." and I introduced him to the other inmates one by one, and they came over and shook hands with him. I showed him where we were starting our reading of a short prayer in English. All of us were reading in unison. I looked at the back of the room and I saw Leopold Licht crying like a baby. No one paid any attention to him because we all knew exactly how he felt. All of us had similar reactions in coming to this group for the first time.

When we concluded, I put my arm around him and I said, "Leopold, you are at home with friends. We are all Jews here."

The next time I saw him a week later, he called me over to the corner and he said, "Miskin, how can I ever thank you?" He said, "In the last week since I was here I have rethought my whole life. For forty years I didn't want anyone to know that I was a Jew, even though I never denied it. I contributed nothing to the Jewish causes and now, at the moment of most dire need in my entire life, you people have welcomed me with open arms." He said, "You've given me the ability to survive my time in prison. I shall never forget this experience."

On Yom Kippur, Leopold Licht fasted with the rest of the Jews in Lewisburg.

It was very difficult being a Jew in prison. There were many men who took delight in tormenting the average inmate, and these men took even more pleasure in harassing and creating problems for Jewish inmates. For this reason there were some Jews who preferred to put "no religion" on the official forms.

There was one occasion when the Protestant chaplain called me to his office to discuss a situation that had arisen. An inmate had contacted him who said that he was Jewish, but had stated on his questionnaire upon entering Lewisburg that he had "no religion." This man now wanted to be officially recognized as a Jew. The Protestant chaplain asked my opinion. This was a problem that I had not encountered before, but I understood the situation very well because I knew the man involved. I guessed that he had determined in his mind when he came to Lewisburg that it would be easier for him not to be Jewish. Shortly before we were to have our Passover dinner, he decided that he would like to eat some of the good food we were going to have. This was a circumstance I could not allow. The men in my group had all registered as Jews upon entry in Lewisburg. On many occasions they had been given a bad time because of their Jewishness.

I could not have the fellowship and harmony of our group destroyed by someone who had taken the easy road and now only wanted to fill his belly. This was a very delicate situation that the Protestant chaplain and I found us in. Reverend Dominic respected me both as a man and as a leader of the Jewish congregation. He always cooperated with me one hundred percent.

I asked the chaplain, "What proof do we have that this man is Jewish?" I said to him, "I would suggest that you ask this inmate if he has any proof that he is Jewish and then contact me after you have had a meeting with him."

Within a few days Reverend Dominic contacted me and asked for a meeting. He told me, with a smile on his face, that the inmate didn't know what kind of proof was required. He said that the inmate told him that his father and mother were Jewish and that he had gone to a synagogue as a boy in New York. Beyond that he had no further proof. I warned the chaplain that we had to be very careful because this could be a precedent-setting case. In the future there could be many men who, just prior to Passover, might want to declare themselves Jewish so that they could have the Passover dinner. I didn't have to draw any pictures for Reverend Dominic. He understood the problem. Since we had only about two weeks to go before Passover, I was trying to stall for time. I told Reverend Dominic that without any proof such as letters from a rabbi, I could not take it upon myself to include the inmate in the Passover meal. He had decided upon entering Lewisburg that officially he had "no religion."

"I have to assume," I told Reverend Dominic, "that if he wants to become Jewish at this point, technically we have to consider it as a conversion."

Of course, every inmate is entitled to convert from one religion to another, but there are certain procedures that had to be followed, and I lacked the rabbinical authority to handle a conversion. I suggested that Reverend Dominic take the matter up with our rabbi on his next visit to ascertain for the future what the procedures were for conversion.

Reverend Dominic must have swept the whole thing under the rug and forgotten about it, because the subject was not brought to my attention again.

RESPONSIBILITIES OF LEADERSHIP

Each year in Lewisburg, in the fall, the Jewish community awaited the coming of the High Holy Days, which for orthodox Jews is the culmination of all religious activities during the years. The authorities gave those inmates officially classified as Jewish time off and facilities to use for our prayer services.

On the day of Yom Kippur, orthodox Jews throughout the world fast for twenty-four hours. During the fast not only do observant Jews abstain from food, they do not drink any liquids nor do they smoke. Many of us in Lewisburg abstained in the orthodox manner. I, as the leader of the Jewish community, felt that I had to do what the most orthodox did, even though I had never fasted on the outside. It is difficult enough to fast on the outside in such a way. In prison, where an inmate is subjected to so many pressures, it doesn't take much imagination to understand that to refrain from smoking, for a heavy smoker, is in itself a supreme sacrifice. By fasting, we would not go to the mess hall for two meals, breakfast and lunch. As poor as the food was, mealtimes were the big events of the day and to give up meals voluntarily took considerable strength of character.

By orthodox law, we could not eat until after sundown. By sundown the evening meal had already been served to the other inmates. The authorities made special arrangements for us to eat the same meal served to the other inmates, but it was served a little later. The only way that I could give an accurate count of the men who would be entitled to the late meal was to include the total Jewish population. Therefore, if an inmate wanted to, he could go to the mess hall for the regular meal and then have an extra meal with us later in the evening. This was something that I felt I could not allow. I realized that I was assuming dictatorial powers, but I demanded of my men that orthodox or not, they would not go into the mess hall with the other inmates that day, period. I didn't dictate to them that they had to fast, because that is a personal decision to be made by each Jew. If they wanted to eat their personal candies or cookies in their cells while they missed their meals, that was their decision and none of my business. The burden of my responsibility as leader of the Jewish group in cases such as this was not in dealing with matters of religion. There were other problems that I had to face and solve in order to eliminate any accusations of privilege from the officials or inmates. I had to forestall any possible charges that our religious observances and holidays were a phony gimmick to enable us to fill our bellies and get an extra meal. I had proven to the officials the trustworthiness of my group on many occasions and of my personal responsibility in any of our extra-curricular activities. It was very important that we maintained unity. To the best of my knowledge during the several years that I was the leader of the group, no Jew entered the mess hall on Yom Kippur day.

    I arrived at the position of president of the Jewish group in Lewisburg by fluke. I didn't want the job. I felt that I was totally unqualified for it, but I had the responsibility thrust on me by circumstance. At the time I was elected vice-president, I felt the job was only an honorary position and that my duties would be negligible. In the past the president had handled everything. Little did I dream that shortly after my election the president would be transferred to another institution.

Before another election could take place, which had to be officially sanctioned by our visiting rabbi, the rabbi himself moved to another part of the United States. We were without a rabbi for months and I was the *de facto* leader of the Jews in our walled city.

The primary reason that my religious knowledge was so limited was due to my father's attitude towards religion. He had been raised in an orthodox orphanage in Minsk, Russia. When he came to the United States, married and had children, he determined that he would not stuff religion down his children's throats the way it had been done to him. He taught me a great love for and responsibility towards my people, but I lacked formal religious training and practice. When I found myself in my position of leadership, I felt as if I were carrying a mountain on my back. I was well aware of the responsibilities and burdens that were mine and I felt qualified in handling my duties in every way but the religious aspect. I then determined that I would learn as much about my religion as I could, under the circumstances. Through the Protestant chaplain I received all the books on Judaism I needed. I read every book I could find in the library on the history of the Jews, orthodox practices, and Zionism. I read every word on every page in the Old Testament and the New Testament. I was still greatly lacking in the knowledge I felt a man in my position should have, but by the time I left Lewisburg I no longer felt unqualified for my job.

I took my responsibilities very seriously and the burdens of assisting my co-religionists in their survival in the Lewisburg jungle became so heavy that I began to feel as if I were the leader of the Jews in the Warsaw Ghetto. The problems of my fellow Jews became my problems. I have no doubt that the time, the effort, and the emotion I put into doing my job assisted me more than I can understand, even now, in surviving mentally and emotionally through those difficult years.

One of the most unpleasant tasks that befell me as leader of my Jewish group was in connection with the death of a young man from Ohio by the name of Levin. He was in his early twenties. He was a short, fat, good-humored fellow, who was always good company. His sentence was for a year and a day for a business related crime. He had never been in prison before, and probably never even had a traffic ticket offense in his life.

He asked my advice one day as to whether or not he should have his tonsils removed in our hospital. I asked him, "Do you have to take them out?"

He said, "Well, the doctors here have told me that there is no emergency, but they advised if I don't take care of it now I should within a few months after I get out."

I said, "When are you due to leave?" He had perhaps two months left to do. I said to him, "My friend, if it's not an emergency, wait until you get home."

He said, "I've been told the doctors are very good here."

I said, "To the best of my knowledge, they are. But wait until you get home."

He said, "Well, the way I look at it, my last couple of months will be broken up by my stay in the hospital, and when I get back to Ohio, I don't have to mess around with surgery. I can go right back to my business. It'll be so much easier that way."

I said, "Do whatever you think is right. You know your situation."

He said, "I think I will do it."

Within several hours after his surgery, he was dead. I later learned that he had come through surgery all right, but died because of negligence in his post-operative care. In a prison hospital, inmates handle all the duties other than those performed by the doctors. Some inmates take their duties more seriously than others. The man who was supposed to watch Levin during the post-operative period was not what he should have been, and Levin died.

His death would have been painful enough to all of us had things been handled properly, but they were not. When I heard of his death, I immediately contacted the Protestant chaplain to see what arrangements were being made to ship Levin's body back to Ohio, and to find out about the necessary religious services. The chaplain hadn't even been notified of Levin's death. He made some inquiries for me and told me that Levin's body had been taken to a local undertaker for embalming. I was shocked. No one in any religious capacity had been contacted. I asked the chaplain what the procedures would have been if a dead inmate were Protestant or Catholic. He told me that the chaplain would have been notified as soon as it was felt that death was imminent so that the proper religious ritual would be followed. The Protestant chaplain and I were good friends so I could speak candidly to him. I wanted to know why I, as leader of the Jewish group, had not been notified so that a rabbi in a neighboring town could have been consulted. He didn't have an answer. I requested of him to set up an immediate meeting for me with the warden. The warden was not available, but I spoke with the associate warden. He agreed that there should have been provision made for a Jewish inmate.

I asked him, "Warden, do you mean to say that you have no directives from the Federal Bureau of Prisons in Washington as to what should be done if an inmate of the Jewish faith dies?"

He said, "No, I have none."

I told him in very plain words that this was disgraceful. He assured me that he agreed with me and that he would contact Washington himself without delay and make sure that there was a definite directive established for the future. He asked me what procedure I would have followed had I been contacted immediately.

I told him, "I don't know. I am not qualified. But there are rabbis who are qualified, and they would let me know what procedures to follow." I also indicated to him that frequently among orthodox Jews, embalming is not practiced.

Within a few days I was called up several times by both the Protestant chaplain and the associate warden and was shown physical evidence that the Federal Prison headquarters in Washington, D.C., which had been remiss in this area for so many years, did in fact establish procedures to be followed in case of the death of a Jewish inmate.

PASSOVER

As the Passover holiday drew near in Lewisburg, we started making our preparations. The Protestant chaplain was notified ahead of time that the holiday was approaching and he, in turn, notified the kitchen staff. The menu was always the same, the traditional meal of chopped liver, chicken soup, matzoh balls, chicken, and matzoh. The Passover meal was always held approximately two hours later than the main chow line in the mess hall. The Passover Seder should be held at sundown. However, due to the unique problems in prison, we had to give the kitchen staff time to finish feeding the other inmates and also to clean up the facilities. Since there were usually no more than fifteen to twenty of us, it was not a big job of preparation for the kitchen staff.

Most of the planning that I had to do as leader of the Jewish congregation was the determination of what portions of the Passover service we would conduct. The majority of us were not orthodox and we didn't want to go through the whole *Haggadah*. Also, due to the time limitations placed on us in the mess hall, we had to be in and out for security reasons within a given time. Since most of the Jewish men were in for short sentences, each year a large percentage of the men had not been there the previous Passover. Jews traditionally are independent thinkers. There are three main branches of Judaism – orthodox, conservative, and reform – and within each branch there are diversified opinions as to how things should be conducted. It was no different in Lewisburg. Out of our tiny population, we generally had fifteen or twenty individual opinions.

Although I was the leader of this religious group and made the final determination on all questions pertaining to religion or survival, I couldn't read Hebrew. Therefore, I had to rely on other inmates, not only for the service conducted at the Passover meal, but for the weekly Saturday service, as well. It was very fortuitous that I was never without someone who could read Hebrew fluently. As one inmate would leave, and everyone began to get apprehensive about who would fill his shoes, lo and behold, a new inmate would come in who would know at least as much as the previous one.

There was one member of our group who took

great pleasure in leading us in our Jewish services and who felt that the importance of doing it properly was his personal responsibility. I determined to give him the honor of being our chief Hebrew reader at the Passover Seder. This man was Kohen with a K. I made my decision very hesitantly because I felt sure that anything Kohen with a K was involved in could not go smoothly. He would have to antagonize someone along the way or create problems of some sort. It could be no other way. Yet, since this post was so extremely important to him, and my other colleagues who could read Hebrew were not offended, I chose Kohen with a K to be our leader.

Because of the starkness of our existence in Lewisburg, the meaning of the Passover dinner and Seder became very, very important. It represented everything that we did not have in Lewisburg. Collectively, we worked many hours in advance of the holidays in practice sessions to assure that the assigned portions would be read in a proper and timely manner. Each man knew his passage. There was no lapse in time between readers and both the English and Hebrew portions were read fluently.

There was one other preparation that could only be done within the last couple of days before Passover – the chopped liver. Through the cooperation of the Protestant chaplain and my many contacts on the supervisory staff in the kitchen, I worked out a system. We would collect all of the chicken livers from the chickens that were used to feed the general population and save them for our Passover dinner. The Passover season, of course, comes very close to the Easter season, at which time chicken is served to the general inmate population. If there is an inmate population of fifteen hundred men and an official staff of approximately five hundred, and each man gets one-half of a chicken (regardless of how small the chicken might be), there would be one thousand chicken livers. That makes a lot of chopped liver. Of course, the existence of this delicacy was no secret, and after the chopped liver was made a certain percentage always mysteriously disappeared. As in the case of not being able to read Hebrew but having other men in my group who could, in making the chopped liver I was in the same situation. I didn't know how to make it, but there were always men in my group who swore they were the greatest chopped liver makers in the world. We would receive a special pass for about six of us to work late one night in the kitchen to prepare the chopped liver.

As the day of Passover drew near, the emotions of the Jewish group heightened in anticipation of the lovely ceremony that would remind each of the men of Passovers celebrated with their families in the past and of the delicacies each one had waited so long to taste. On the first day of Passover we had all gathered in our meeting place before going down to the mess hall to partake of the Seder and dinner. As the men were coming into the room, each with his inmate clothing recently washed and looking as neat as he could make himself, one of my men burst into the room and said, "Guess what happened to Kohen with a K?"

I said, "What?"

He said, "He's in the hole."

I said, "My God, what happened?" And I was told he was put in the hole for being involved in a fight.

In Lewisburg the innocent party to a fight is punished just as severely as the one who started the fight. As the guards approach, they are both immediately put into the hole for further determination of what the punishment is to be. It is always impossible to learn the truth about any prison fight, so the policy is equal punishment for all participants. Since we all knew Kohen with a K, none of us was terribly surprised. He was an old man with a big mouth whom I had kept from harm on many occasions, and finally the inevitable happened. I was told that he was not injured, that it was a minor scuffle with no serious consequences.

Everyone suggested that I immediately go to see the Protestant chaplain and the warden to get him out of the hole. I explained to my men that I doubted very seriously if I could get him out, even with my influence and even with the fact that this was the first night of Passover, and as an orthodox Jew this night had extreme importance to him. The most important need to get him out of the hole was the fact that he was our Hebrew reader and we had practiced with him for several weeks. After analyzing the pros and cons of this crisis, I determined that it would be a bad move on my part to attempt to intervene in such a situation. In all probability, I couldn't help anyway. I had turned my thoughts to the dilemma of how to replace Kohen with a K, when up jumped my friend Mendel Moskowitz, who put his arm around me and told me that my problems were over. Mendel was a man of many talents, but also a man of many lies. Most of the accomplishments he laid claim to were so impossible and so ridiculous as to insult one's intelligence. However, on many occasions, to the surprise of all, he proved that he could, indeed, do what he said he could do.

I looked at Moskowitz and I said, "Please. This is too important a time to give me a lot of bullshit."

With a hurt look on his face, he said, "I am serious. I read Hebrew beautifully. I am much better than Kohen with a K."

I asked him, "Moskowitz, in all this time that you have been coming to services, why didn't you ever tell me?"

He answered, "You never asked me and there were always other guys who could do it. You didn't need me. Now you need me. I will take care of all your problems. It will be beautiful. Don't worry about a thing."

My back was against the wall. I had no other reader. I said, "Moskowitz, if you don't know what you are doing, tell me now, for God's sake. There are men in the group who can stumble through it. Do you really know what the hell you are doing?"

He said, "Don't worry about a thing. I guarantee you it will be perfect."

And to the surprise and relief of all concerned he conducted the best service at our Seder that we ever had.

THE LIGHTER SIDE

The meetings held by the Jewish inmates were not always serious and religious in nature. Amongst us we always had men who were fascinating talkers and very humorous.

One of the funniest and most touching scenes I ever witnessed took place one Sunday morning as we were gathering for our Sunday meeting. One of the men in our group was Jake Meisa (nicknamed Bubba), a small-time gambler from Washington, D.C. He was just a little larger than the average jockey. He was always good for a racetrack story or a tale about a suspense-filled poker game. On this particular morning I was talking with Jake when the contingent from quarantine entered the room. The first to enter was Benny Ruby, whom I had met and interviewed when he first arrived a few days previously. He was a man in his sixties, large and fat, with a very sad look on his face. Benny was a very successful businessman from Baltimore, Maryland, who had been convicted of a white-collar crime.

As he entered the room, he stopped dead in

his tracks and said, "Jake!"

Jake, who was talking to me, turned around, looked at Benny, and cried, "Benny!"

Simultaneously, they both said to each other, "What are you doing here?" By this time they had gotten much closer and were hugging each other.

I said to both of them, "Obviously, you know each other."

Jake looked at me and said, "That's my brother-in-law."

I said, "Your brother-in-law?"

He said, "Yeah."

They finally cleared up my confusion by telling me that neither of them had known that the other had been in difficulties with the law. In each case, it had been a close family secret. Since Washington and Baltimore are about forty miles distant, the secret was easily kept. Can you imagine the shock each one felt on seeing the other in a federal penitentiary? After a few minutes, they went into a corner and gossiped like two old women for the remainder of our Sunday meeting.

There was always an interesting or funny incident that had happened to one of our group, and we all looked forward to each Sunday to be brought up to date.

We had one inmate who was a compulsive gambler. Gambling was an obsession with Izzy Schwartz. Although gambling is strictly forbidden in prison because of the serious problems that could develop between winners and losers, this was not enough to stop Izzy. He would gamble on whether people would make parole or how long it would take before someone would be sent to the hole. Handball games were a constant source of action for him. The big leagues for Izzy was his own football pool, which he developed using his own point spread. He was the king bookmaker for football action in all of Lewisburg, and he knew his business. Since money is not available for gambling in a prison, cigarettes are the coin of the realm. Izzy had more cigarettes than he knew what to do with. Since inmates were prohibited from having more than two cartons in their possession at any time, Izzy would have various friends hold his cigarettes for him. On one Sunday morning as I was ready to start our meeting, I noticed that Izzy was not present. I asked the men if they knew why he was not present, since he was always at the Sunday meetings. I was told that just the night before he had voluntarily checked into solitary confinement.

Solitary is a most unpleasant experience, and most of the time it is only used as severe punishment. However, Izzy had a very good reason for voluntarily requesting that he be put there. On his latest football pool, everything had gone wrong. His analysis of the potential scores was a disaster. He had debts to pay among the hundreds of inmates who had placed bets with him that amounted to hundreds of cartons of cigarettes. There was no way that he could ever pay the debts because of the limitation of twelve dollars per month allowed for commissary spending. Even if he called in all the cigarettes he had loaned to his friends and borrowed as much as he could from his close friends, he could not pay off. There was only one way he could save his life, and that was to spend the remainder of his sentence in solitary confinement. He openly confessed to the authorities what his problem was and why he needed protection and the prison officials understood his situation thoroughly. There was no need to discipline him for violating the rules against gambling. They had to save his life first. For the benefit of all concerned, he was transferred to another institution shortly afterwards.

We, of course, always had our friend Mendel Moskowitz, who was always available to entertain us at the drop of a hat. His stories were endless. We all felt that his stories were barefaced lies, but you never knew for sure. He was such an extraordinary person that any of his stories could have been true. He told us in detail of how General Eichelberger, commanding officer of the Eighth Army in Japan after World War II, personally requested a meeting with him. Then Eichelberger gave Moskowitz the civilian rank of colonel to design the vault systems for the Bank of Japan. His countless stories indicating his expertise as a diamond appraiser were always interesting. He gave us detail upon detail of the year that he won the A.A.U. wrestling championship of New York City. Perhaps some of his most entertaining stories dealt with his worldwide fame as a dice tester, and how some of the largest crap games in New York City had been temporarily held up until the arrival of Mendel Moskowitz to test the dice. His stories and exploits were limitless. Although frequently we would become disgusted and annoyed at his going a bit too far and wild in his storytelling, we all enjoyed them because he was, in fact, a master storyteller.

TRACK FEVER

Hymie was a member of our Jewish group. When he came to Lewisburg he wasn't exactly skinny, but he certainly was slight of build. Hymie's job assignment was in the officers' mess. This was an envied position. The officers, naturally, ate much better food than the inmates, and Hymie ate the same food he served the officers. By the change in his appearance from month to month, as he gained pound after pound, it was obvious to all of us that he was eating well and frequently. Hymie liked food and he liked feeling fat. He was also lazy.

One day, to my surprise, I noticed Hymie running the track in our exercise yard. He could hardly stumble around the track, but he kept going. The next day he ran again. Every day he ran the track from the first whistle, which was after breakfast on Saturday and Sunday, until the yard was cleared out in time for dinner. Hymie ran the track without talk, without noticing anyone, like a man in a trance. He became a fixture in the exercise yard. You always knew that you would find

Hymie running the track. It became my firm belief, and the belief of others who knew him well, that there could be only one reason why a lazy fat man like Hymie would run the track with such concentration and diligence. He was going to attempt an escape and he was preparing for that day so that when he got past the wall, through one method or another, he would be in proper condition to run as far and as fast as necessary. After many months went by, I was totally convinced that this was his purpose, but I was afraid to ask him. You learn in prison not to ask certain questions. If he was planning an escape, I didn't want to know about it.

One day, as suddenly as he started running, he stopped running, and he ran no more. I asked him why he had stopped running. His answer was so obvious that we all missed it.

He said, "Hell, I was getting as fat as a hog." He said, "Now I look great. I have accomplished my purpose and I don't have to run anymore. I'm going up for parole shortly, and I might make it."

THE LEWISBURG UNITED JEWISH APPEAL

The Jewish group in Lewisburg, due to our small numbers, our mutual reliance, our common background, and the time spent together at services and meetings, became a very close unit. When it came to our attention that some of us were without cigarettes, it was only natural that those with cigarettes would share them during a meeting. There were men amongst us who had no money to spend at the commissary, some because they had no family on the outside and some because they did not want their family to know they were in prison. A limitation of twelve dollars a month meant that a heavy smoker, after purchasing cigarettes, toothpaste, razor blades, and other necessary odds and ends, had no money left to buy the goodies that were available at the commissary. In prison it was unheard of for an inmate to give cigarettes to someone else without receiving any benefit in return. It was extremely difficult for a smoker to endure the stress of prison life without the small comfort a cigarette can offer.

The Jewish group at Lewisburg was, for all

practical purposes, an isolated world within a world. In many respects we looked to the history of our people, not only to teach us survival techniques, but to set us an example of how to care for one another, in many ways. We developed our own United Jewish Appeal.

It was understood that each Jewish inmate would voluntarily contribute two packs of cigarettes each month to the welfare fund. Any inmate who had no money in his commissary fund was entitled to receive two packs each week when he came to services. Fortunately for us, the number of inmates who relied upon our war chest was seldom more than one or two at any time. We all derived such satisfaction from sharing our cigarettes with those in our group who had none that we determined to go one step further.

The federal prison system has a far-flung, elaborate network of prison facilities throughout the United States. Prisoners are constantly being transferred from one institution to another. The federal prison buses, used for transporting prisoners, have the exterior appearance of a regular Greyhound bus, but on the inside are manned by two armed guards in addition to the driver. Inmates are securely handcuffed during transportation and the buses do not travel at night. There are enough institutions scattered around the United States so that a prison bus can go from one institution to another during the daylight hours, and the inmates are housed at a federal facility overnight. Therefore, in Lewisburg we were constantly having new prisoners in transit in the quarantine area. Quarantine is difficult under any circumstances. Those inmates quarantined in transit are restricted even more. Some men only spend one night. However, under certain circumstances it might be a two week stay-over.

We determined that any Jews who came into Lewisburg in transit would also receive the benefit of our United Jewish Appeal cigarette fund. I have no doubt that this was the first time in the annals of penology that a prisoner, stopping in transit at a penitentiary, received cigarettes from any inmate group. Our undertaking was so novel in its concept and so gratifying that we all cooperated enthusiastically in making it work.

Normally, new inmates are interviewed and information is passed on to the chaplains as to religious preference. The transient inmates' files never left the quarantine area and the chaplains were not notified, although these men were entitled to attend religious services. The public address system announced the time of services and the transients went in a separate group. It was very difficult to determine if and when Jewish inmates were in the transient area. Most transients have many problems on their minds and a large percentage are not interested in any religious activity. Jews finding themselves in a strange prison frequently are wary about being the only inmate in a cellblock to request to go to Jewish services.

I had to develop a system through my many contacts to determine who was Jewish in the transient quarantine group. The records of the transients were carried on each federal bus and left with the institution while the men were kept in quarantine. As a man departed on a different bus, his records went with him in the possession of the lieutenant in charge of the bus. The only inmate who had access to the records was the clerk typist who worked in the quarantine area.

Trading favors between inmates in different jobs is a way of life in prison. The clerk typist in the quarantine area was approached and requested to supply me with the names of any newly arrived Jewish inmate. Since the number of inmates arriving at any one time was very limited, it was a simple matter for him to check the file for the religion of each man. The Protestant chaplain was always cooperative about issuing me a pass to visit a Jewish inmate. Oddly enough, no one ever asked me how I knew that a transient inmate was Jewish. I knew that if the officials wanted proof that the inmate was a Jew, the files would verify the fact.

It was always extremely interesting to meet a newly arrived inmate. I would introduce myself, explain my position in the Jewish congregation, and offer him two packs of cigarettes. I would explain that it was the policy of the Jewish inmate group in Lewisburg to give two packs of cigarettes to every Jew who came through in transit. Whether or not the inmate was a hardened con or a first-timer in prison, he always had a look of total disbelief on his face when I handed him the cigarettes. As these men traveled with the federal bus to the various institutions in the United States, there is no doubt that they spread the word of our United Jewish Appeal fund in Lewisburg.

I have often wondered whether our example

led to the establishment of U.J.A.'s in other federal prisons.

A TALE OF TWO RABBIS

When I first arrived in Lewisburg, Rabbi Pickholtz, who lived in a nearby city, visited the Jewish inmates periodically – not on a regularly scheduled basis. He was a wonderful little man who was gentle and kind and understood perfectly the purpose of being a visiting prison rabbi. He realized that he was not a full-time chaplain as were the Protestant and Catholic chaplains, and his only purpose in coming to Lewisburg whenever he was able – usually once or twice a month – was to offer comfort through his personality to these sad men. He was perhaps about five feet four inches, thin, with a trim little mustache.

Upon entering the room, he would extend his hand to whoever was nearby and say, "Hello Abe, how's your bad feet? Hello Jake, how do you like your new job? Hello Sam, your wife tells me you're feeling much better."

When the rabbi came, our meeting room took on the atmosphere of a gathering in a delicatessen in New York's East Side. Everyone was relaxed, and everyone loved to see Rabbi Pickholtz. After a few minutes of handshaking, he would say, "O.K., I'm going next door. Anybody that wants to talk to me, come on in."

There was no formality whatsoever and what the men generally wanted to talk to him about were personal family matters. One man hadn't heard from his wife and he would ask the rabbi to please contact her. Another was worried about his child's operation. There were very few official Lewisburg related matters connected with his visits. This was not his job and he made no pretense of being tied in with the prison authorities. On occasion, when there was need, he did intercede and see the warden for some problem that required his direct contact. For an inmate to meet and chat with a person who is not an inmate and yet is not part of the official structure of the prison is a relaxing and warm and needed break in the routine. Rabbi Pickholtz understood these things very well, and he contributed to the welfare of the men so very much just by being natural and being himself. Unfortunately, after about two years from the time of my coming to Lewisburg, he left his synagogue in nearby Pennsylvania and moved to a different part of the country. There was a long period when we had no rabbi, and he was missed greatly.

One day I received notice from the Protestant chaplain that our new rabbi, Rabbi Werner Reicher, would be meeting with us the following Sunday. I notified my flock quickly and we were eager to meet him. The first meeting was quite a disillusionment. As was the usual procedure, our group numbering from fifteen to twenty men was milling around the classroom in the education department having personal conversations, when the rabbi walked in. An inmate who has served any length of time at all, in order to survive, quickly becomes an observer of human nature, and it didn't take a Sherlock Holmes to detect that this man was not like the warm and helpful Rabbi Pickholtz. He entered the room brusquely, looked us over with cold eyes, marched to the podium, laid his briefcase on the desk, and stood without saying a word until all was quiet in the room. He then directed us all to move down to the front rows of seats. He announced who he was and that he would be our visiting rabbi in the future. He had prepared a resumé of his background, which he proudly handed out. The resumé indicated that he was born in Germany and held a PhD in Theology and it listed his published works.

He announced the procedures that would be followed in the future.

We would meet on alternate Sundays at a given hour, at which time he would conduct services. When an inmate felt the necessity of speaking to the rabbi privately, he was to submit an interview slip in advance to the Protestant chaplain, state his reasons, the problem, and what he wanted the rabbi to do on his behalf. He stated that since there was a limited amount of time, he would only interview those men where, in his opinion, there would be merit in a personal interview. Otherwise, the request would be answered in writing.

When he had finished with his announcement, he said, "Let us begin on page such and such."

All of us in the room looked at one another in total disbelief. We were sick. This was to be our leader in the future and our contact with the outside world! As inmates, we realized that he was not a man to offend or anger. It was obvious that he felt he was part of the official prison administration and that we were convicts. To him our purpose in coming to these services was only to be present while he conduced religious services. This closely-knit Jewish group that had survived for so long through the aid of one another and through my leadership and the assistance and good will of Rabbi Pickholtz, was about to be shattered. After a brief service, he announced that since this was his first time here he would not require written notices in advance and asked if anyone wished to see him. No one did. However, I felt that I should have a private conversation with him.

 We went into the private room next door. I explained to him what my position was as leader of the Jewish group and of the past procedures that had been followed as far as my relationship with Rabbi Pickholtz was concerned. I told him that during the period when we had no rabbi the Protestant chaplain had recognized me as the Jew in authority. In a very cold answer he indicated that he saw no reason to change anything. However, any questions of importance he wanted channeled through the Protestant chaplain, who would contact him for instructions. I felt as an inmate that I did not want to offend or tangle with this man. I felt also that possibly he could harm me in some way. I respectfully thanked him for his cooperation and we ended our meeting.

Months went by and the attendance at the Sunday meetings dwindled to only a handful. His routine never varied. He maintained his official cold stance and even though our Jewish group continued its cohesiveness through the Saturday services, when he was not present, the lack of our Sunday social meeting was showing its effect. It was not that he hampered our activities in any way because we could meet on the Sundays he was not present. However, his attitude and presence took the heart from us. We were much better off without any rabbi than having one who filled so little of our needs. I had worked so long and hard on behalf of the Jewish group in Lewisburg and I understood the needs of this group so very well. I finally made the decision that it was my duty to have a heart to heart talk with this man, even if I antagonized him greatly. After much thought I concluded that my relationship with the officials of the institution was strong enough and I had proven my worthiness enough so that even if the rabbi were to report me for insubordination, the harm to me would be small. I sent in an interview slip requesting a meeting with Rabbi Reicher, according to his instructions, and explained in the letter that my need for the meeting was not personal, but it involved the good and welfare of the total Jewish community in Lewisburg and I felt it extremely important that I be granted this time.

When we met I looked at him for a long period before I spoke, and I said, to him, "Rabbi, I carry a terrible burden on my shoulders, and I don't know how to handle it. From your resumé and from the way you conduct yourself, I have no doubt that you are a very intelligent, very well educated man. I hope that if I offend you in what I am about to say, you will forgive me because I am not doing this for any personal gain or with any malice in my heart toward you."

I said, "I know that you escaped from the Nazis in Germany. You of all people must realize the need of fellowship amongst Jews in times of stress. Here in Lewisburg we maintain our sanity and survive by the camaraderie and the assistance we give each other. I realize that Rabbi Pickholtz and you are two different kinds of men with different methods and I wouldn't anticipate that you would both do things the same way. However, I feel it is my duty to convey to you the great harm you're doing to your fellow Jews here in Lewisburg. I assume and I pray that you are unaware of how your conduct has demoralized us. As an inmate I realize very strongly my fragile position in discussing these matters with you. But I am a leader of my men here. I was elected through a democratic process and I have served them diligently and effectively for several years. I know the needs of these men."

I then paused to regroup my thoughts and I looked at his face. He had not said one word and I assumed he was unaccustomed to having anyone, inmate or otherwise, speak to him so directly and so personally.

I said, "Rabbi, perhaps you can't help yourself. I don't know. My father always told me that German Jews were different from other Jews and I always laughed. I assumed that this was the traditional feeling of Eastern European Jews about German Jews. Perhaps he was right. We have a very harsh and ugly existence here. We have officials on our necks twenty-four hours a day. You are our one contact with the outside world and with Judaism. We don't need a rabbi to lead us in our services. We have many able men who can do that. We need a warm, friendly, understanding Jew who comes from the outside world and shows us with warmth that someone cares. A pat on the back, a concern about our families, an interest in our medical problems... those are the things we need from you. I think that your initial mistake, Rabbi, and I do assume that your intentions are to do the best job possible, but the initial mistake was not meeting with me and asking me what you could do to help these men. I would have explained their needs to you. You have noticed, I am sure, that the attendance has dwindled consistently. You must have wondered why. You conduct yourself like a storm trooper in there, and that we don't need. You request an interview slip a week in advance. That's what the warden does. I realize you have a limited amount of time. What you should do when you first come in is ask how many men want to see you. If there are a large number, eliminate the prayers. If there is a small number, take care of each one immediately. If there are too many men who want to see you in the time you have available, the men themselves will determine which are the emergency cases and which can wait. Please, Rabbi, I beg you, show these men some warmth. Show them friendship. Show them personal interest. Don't call them by their last names. Call them by their first names. Ask them if there is anything you can do for them."

When I had finished, we both sat in silence for a long time. Then, slowly, he answered me.

He said, "First of all I do want to state that German Jews are no different than other Jews. If I have acted differently from Rabbi Pickholtz, it is because I am a different type of man. I will have to think over very carefully all the things you have said, and I realize the difficulty that you had in deciding to come to speak to me." He said, "I don't know if I can change in the way that you feel I should. However, there are certain things that I will immediately rectify, and the first is the requirement for an interview slip. I will attempt to be the rabbi that these men need and whether I succeed or not, we shall see. You must realize, Miskin, that I cannot change the man that I am, whether I am likable or not."

We ended our meeting. I conveyed to my group briefly our discussion. In the future he, indeed, attempted to change what was possible for him to change. It was not long after that he left the position of rabbi at Lewisburg.